D0127224

THE ZUCCHINI HOUDINI

THE ZUCCHINI HOUDINI

BRENDA STANLEY

Bonneville Books
Springville, Utah

ISBN 13: 978-1-59955-427-3

Published by Bonneville Books, an imprint of Cedar Fort, Inc., 2373 W. 700 S., Springville, UT 84663
Distributed by Cedar Fort, Inc., www.cedarfort.com

LIBRARY OF CONGRESS CATALOGING-IN-PUBLICATION DATA
Stanley, Brenda, 1964-
  The zucchini houdini / Brenda Stanley.
    p. cm.
  ISBN: 978-1-59955-427-3 (acid-free paper)
  Cookery (Zucchini)

TX803.Z82 S83 2010
641.6/562 22

        2010013375

Cover and page design by Megan Whittier
Cover design © 2010 by Lyle Mortimer
Edited by Melissa J. Caldwell

Printed in the United States of America

10 9 8 7 6 5 4 3 2 1

Printed on acid-free paper

DEDICATION

To my Grandma Beulah, my Grandma Dorothy,
and my mother, Beverly—
these ladies taught me to cook and love zucchini.

And to my husband, Dave,
who was such a willing and wonderful taste tester!

CONTENTS

INTRODUCTION

The zucchini is a wonderful thing. Ever since I was a little girl, I've loved it. In our garden I would help my father sow seeds in four or five large mounds of dirt. And the most wonderful thing happened just a few weeks later—sprouts. And then a few weeks after that—success! We enjoyed that perfectly shaped, tender, sweet squash all fried up and seasoned just right. Never a year went by that we didn't enjoy those succulent green wonders.

As an adult, I have a similar experience each spring and summer. The only difference is I see what I chose to overlook as a child: the excess. Rare is the gardener who grows zucchini and doesn't end up with too many. I marvel at the way zucchini can turn from a firm, thin, perfectly shaped fruit to a blob the size of a harbor seal in what seems like a few hours.

And that is where my adventure began. I found that if I picked my zucchini at the perfect time, I had bushels. And yet if I waited, even a day or so, I ended up with monsters. So I set out to find ways to enjoy zucchini regardless of the quantity or the size. I interviewed family, friends, and even strangers, asking for their suggestions, stories, and recipes. I attended festivals and farmers' markets to glean ideas. I researched the Internet and found blogs and entire websites dedicated to our long emerald friend.

Zucchini is a versatile, delicious, and plentiful fruit. There are so many ways to use and enjoy these tasty green wonders, and so much to learn about the misunderstood and enormously underappreciated gem of the squash world. Zucchini is commonly thought of as a vegetable; however, by strict definition the zucchini is a fruit because it is the swollen ovary of the zucchini flower. Its flavor is light and sweet with flesh that is tender but firm.

So bring on the large, the plentiful, and even misshapen. I've found that with some creative, simple, and healthy techniques, I could not only use all my zucchini, but also enjoy them and even disguise them in ways that would make anyone sit up and say, "Yum!" I hope that through these delicious and easy recipes, you will learn to love zucchini as much I as do.

HISTORY

Summer squashes, as well as winter squashes, are native to the Americas and belong to the family of Cucurbita. Archaeologists have traced their origins to Mexico, dating back from 7000 to 5500 BCE, when they were an integral part of the ancient diet of maize, beans, and squashes. That pre-Columbian food trio is still the mainstay of the Mexican cuisine and is known today as the "three sisters." Many explorers who came to the Americas took home what they considered strange foods. George Washington and Thomas Jefferson were also squash enthusiasts and enjoyed growing them.

While squash has been popular in the United States since the time of the Pilgrims, zucchini is the most common squash grown today and has only been popular in the United States for the last fifty years. Squash and pumpkins were a popular food source for the early American settlers, but it was not until the nineteenth century that they were accepted as such in Europe. (Europeans originally used them as livestock feed.) While the zucchini has been popular in Italy for over three hundred years, it did not gain widespread recognition in North America until the 1950s.

WHAT'S IN A NAME?

Many names have been given to this squash. Its Latin name is *Cucurbita pepo*. The Italians call it *zucchino*. The French call it *courgette*, a name that has been adopted by the English. The English also refer to a variety that is slightly larger and plumper as *marrow*. The colonists of New England adopted the name *squash*, a word derived from several Native American words for the vegetable, which meant "something eaten raw."

GROWING

Zucchini grow most commonly in cylindrical shapes, but they also grow in round and intermediate shapes. Color varies from a green so dark that it is almost black, to lighter shades of green both with and without stripes, and all the way to various tones of yellow.

Many are highlighted with various degrees of speckling or striping. Cocozelle, a variety of zucchini that originated in Italy, is shorter, plumper, and striped. Today's farmers are developing hybrids that are a visual delight. Some are round, some are yellow, and some are a combination of green and yellow. Others are a cross between zucchini and the fluted patty pan squash.

Zucchini is easy to grow. Some argue that it is too easy. It is a warm season vegetable, but it can be readily injured by frost and freezes. You can plant seeds directly in the garden or use transplants from seeds that were started early indoors. Space plants 24 inches apart on 48-inch wide beds. Hill planting is also feasible. Four to six plants will produce more than enough to feed a family of four in any one growing season. Fertilize as you would for other garden vegetables.

Plants have both male and female flowers, a situation which requires insects (bees primarily) for pollination. If bee activity is low, female flowers are likely to drop. Insects that bother zucchini include leaf miners, aphids, cutworms, squash vine borers, squash bugs, cucumber beetles, mole crickets, and fruit worms.

Common diseases of zucchini are downy mildew, powdery mildew, mosaic viruses, and fruit rots. Occasional injury results from root-knot nematodes.

Crossing with other nearby varieties of squash occurs readily. No harm is done, however, unless the seeds are to be saved and planted. Crossing will occur with straight necks, crooknecks, spaghetti squash, pumpkins, and others.

SO GOOD AND SO GOOD FOR YOU!

With their high water content (more than 95 percent), the zucchini is very low in calories. There are only 13 calories in a half-cup of raw zucchini, with a slight increase to 18 calories in the same amount when cooked. Nutritionally, the zucchini offers valuable antioxidants. They are a good source of fiber with 4 grams per cup, but be sure to include the peel to get all the fiber. Zucchini contain useful amounts of folate (24 mcg/100 g), potassium (280 mg/100 g), vitamin A (384 IU [115 mcg]/100 g), and phosphorus (70 mg). Zucchini are also an excellent source of vitamin C. Dark green zucchini has some beta-carotene, and all types provide small quantities of minerals. The darker the zucchini, the more nutrients it contains. Make sure to wash your zucchini, but don't peel unless the recipe requires it because most of the nutrients are in the skin.

HELPFUL HINTS

Keeping you and your zucchini happy year round

FREEZING

Grate zucchini, drain in a colander, and then pat dry with a paper towel, applying pressure. Remove as much moisture as possible to prevent zucchini from getting soggy when frozen. Place one or two cups of zucchini in freezer bags and seal tightly. It should last for three to four months.

STORING

Store fresh picked or purchased zucchini in a plastic bag in the refrigerator for up to one week for best quality. Be sure the zucchini is dry when you put it in the bag, as moisture will cause mold and spoilage.

COOKING

Zucchini is best if cooked when fresh and small, as it will have more moisture. Steaming produces the crispest, least soggy vegetable. If using zucchini in a casserole recipe, it may be parboiled or steamed to remove some of the moisture. Do not peel unless the recipe specifies to do so.

EQUIVALENTS

1 pound zucchini = 3–4 servings
1 pound zucchini = about 3 medium zucchini
1 pound zucchini = 2½ cups chopped
1 medium zucchini = 1 cup sliced zucchini
1 small zucchini= 4–5 inches long
1 medium zucchini= 6–7 inches long

Anything larger will become bitter tasting and not as desirable. Larger zucchini, however, are perfect for grating and using in baked goods. It is usually necessary to peel large zucchini because the skin becomes tough; however, this removes most of the fiber and nutrients.

After grating zucchini, it is best to let it strain in a colander to remove as much moisture as possible. Squeezing the pulp through paper towels also works well.

BLOSSOMS

Zucchini blossoms are the flowers of the zucchini plant. Male blossoms are best for most recipes. The males don't produce a vegetable but exist to pollinate the females. You can recognize them by their long, straight stems and stamen in the center of each flower. Female blossoms swell at the base, where the zucchini forms, and four little shoots make up the pistil inside. Most recipes tell you to remove the stamens, but it isn't necessary. Handle blossoms carefully and always rinse and pat them dry before use.

GETTING FRESH

So crisp and green, zucchini is perfect in fresh salads and slaws

Zucchini Slaw

Light and fresh, but with a hint of spice.

INGREDIENTS

2 cups zucchini, julienned
1 cup carrots, julienned
½ cup celery, chopped
½ bell pepper, seeded and chopped
½ head red cabbage, grated

⅓ cup olive oil
2 Tbsp. lemon juice
1 tsp. Dijon mustard
¼ tsp. salt
¼ tsp. pepper

SERVES 4

DIRECTIONS

Combine vegetables in a large bowl. In a separate bowl, whisk together the oil, juice, mustard, salt, and pepper. Toss with vegetables and let marinate in fridge for about 30 minutes before serving.

The Zucchini Gets its 15 Minutes of Fame

A quick Internet search reveals that the zucchini is everywhere. There are zucchini dances, zucchini bands, a zucchini land, and even a nativity scene in which the baby Jesus is played by a swaddled zuke. It was the cat versus zucchini fight video that finally made me realize that the zucchini is more than just a prolific green wonder. It is also a media icon. Watch out Oprah.

Creamy Zucchini Cranberry Slaw

This sweet and zesty salad is perfect for summer days.

INGREDIENTS

½ cup buttermilk
½ cup sour cream (fat-free sour cream or plain yogurt can be substituted)
3 Tbsp. honey mustard dressing
3 large carrots, julienned
1 medium zucchini, julienned
½ cup dried cranberries
¼ tsp. salt
¼ tsp. pepper

SERVES
4–6

DIRECTIONS

In a large bowl, whisk together buttermilk, sour cream, and dressing. Add carrots, zucchini, cranberries, salt, and pepper. Mix well. Chill at least an hour.

Asian Zucchini Salad

Even the smell of this fresh salad will make your mouth water.

INGREDIENTS

3 medium zucchini
1 red onion, halved and sliced
¼ cup olive oil
½ tsp. sesame oil
¼ cup rice vinegar
1 Tbsp. soy sauce
2 Tbsp. sesame seeds

SERVES
6

DIRECTIONS

Slice off ends of zucchini and blanch in salted boiling water until tender but still firm. Drain and cut into ½-inch chunks. Place the zucchini and onion in a large bowl. Mix together oils, vinegar, and soy sauce. Toss with zucchini and onion. Sprinkle with sesame seeds. Serve chilled.

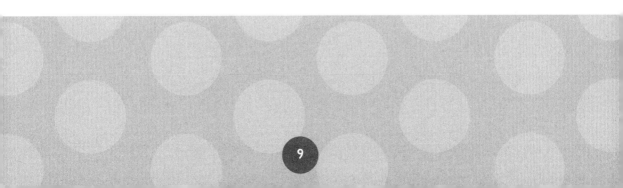

Curried Zucchini Corn Salad

Creamy and full of flavor, this salad is filled with the fresh crunch of garden veggies.

INGREDIENTS

¼ cup olive oil

2 Tbsp. curry powder

2 cloves garlic, crushed

⅓ cup mayonnaise (fat-free can be substituted)

⅓ cup sour cream (fat-free can be substituted)

2 Tbsp. honey

1 Tbsp. lemon juice

1½ tsp. salt

¾ tsp. pepper

2 large red bell peppers

5 medium zucchini

2 Tbsp. olive oil

2 cups canned (drained) or frozen corn

½ cup chopped red onion

SERVES 8

DIRECTIONS

Combine oil, curry, and garlic in a skillet. Sauté until garlic is fragrant. Cool, and discard garlic. In a bowl, whisk together mayonnaise, sour cream, honey, lemon juice, salt, and pepper. Whisk in curry mixture. Set aside. In a large skillet, sauté peppers and zucchini in olive oil until browned and tender. In a large bowl combine curry mixture, zucchini, peppers, and the remaining ingredients. Mix well. Serve chilled.

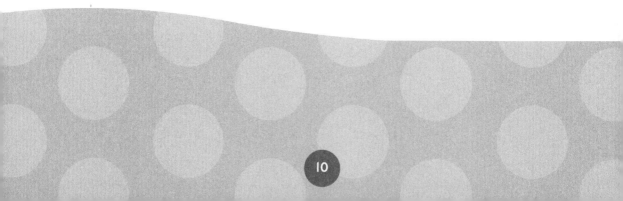

Zucchini Avocado Salad

Smooth and rich—there's no need for a heavy dressing on this summertime salad.

INGREDIENTS

2 cups cubed zucchini
1 Hass avocado, peeled, pitted, and cubed
¼ cup oil
2 Tbsp. lemon juice
1 clove garlic, crushed
¼ tsp. salt

SERVES
4

DIRECTIONS

Steam zucchini for about 4 minutes or until crisp tender. Combine all ingredients in a large bowl. Mix well. Serve well chilled.

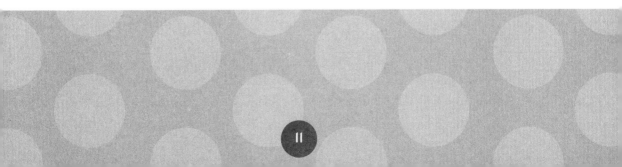

Hot Zucchini Tomato Salad

This salad can be served before dinner or as a side. I also love this for lunch.

INGREDIENTS

1 Tbsp. butter or margarine
2 green onions, finely chopped
⅔ cup cream (fat-free half-and-half can be substituted)
¼ cup chopped fresh basil (or 3 tsp. dried basil)
1 tsp. lemon juice
1 tsp. red wine vinegar
¼ tsp. hot sauce
¼ tsp. salt
⅛ tsp. pepper
2 medium zucchini, sliced thin
2 medium tomatoes, seeded and cubed

SERVES
4

DIRECTIONS

Melt butter in large skillet. Sauté green onions until tender. Add cream and basil. Heat to boiling. Reduce heat and simmer, stirring constantly until sauce thickens. Add lemon juice, vinegar, hot sauce, salt, and pepper. Mix well. Add zucchini and tomatoes, and cook only until coated. Sprinkle with more fresh basil as a garnish.

Zucchini Salad Dressing

The zucchini gives it a fresh crunch.

INGREDIENTS

2 cups peeled and chopped zucchini
½ cup plain yogurt
¼ cup sour cream (fat-free can be substituted)
1 tsp. dill weed
¼ tsp. salt
¼ tsp. pepper
milk

MAKES
2 CUPS

DIRECTIONS

Combine all ingredients and mix well. Use milk for desired consistency.
Store in a sealed container in the refrigerator.

Zucchini Fairies

In small towns everywhere, there is a season that people know well but keep to themselves for fear of being targeted. When the autumn moon is full and the warm breezes feel blissful during the night, the people of these towns spend their evenings locking their doors and windows and closing up their sheds, barns, and garages. They pass by their windows and peer out, wondering if they'll catch a glimpse and stop what they have planned to avoid. It is the only time of year they lock up their lives and peer suspiciously out at night. But most of these people have good reason because they have been hit in the past. They were careless and left a garage door cracked or a shed unlocked. Then, when the morning sun glistened on a warm August day, there they were—bushels of zucchini left by what can only be blamed on the fairies that inhabit the harvest nights. August 8 is Sneak Some Zucchini Onto Your Neighbor's Porch Day.

Spicy Ginger Zucchini Salad

A wonderful mixture of southwest and Asian flavors.

INGREDIENTS

**SERVES
4–6**

1 lime, zest and juice
1 Tbsp. soy sauce
1½ tsp. sesame oil
1½ tsp. finely grated fresh ginger
¼ tsp. crushed red pepper flakes
2 Tbsp. chopped fresh cilantro
3 medium zucchini, julienned

DIRECTIONS

In a large bowl, combine lime zest and juice, soy sauce, sesame oil, ginger, red pepper flakes, and cilantro. Add zucchini and mix well. Chill for 30 minutes.

Italian Zucchini Salad

This is a hearty and zesty salad that I love to serve along with my pasta dishes.

INGREDIENTS

6 small zucchini, julienned
2 cups halved cherry tomatoes
1 cup chopped fresh parsley
¼ cup chopped fresh basil
1 cup cubed mozzarella cheese
½ cup red wine vinegar
¾ cup extra virgin olive oil
¼ tsp. salt
¼ tsp. pepper

SERVES
6

DIRECTIONS

In a large bowl combine zucchini, tomatoes, parsley, basil, and cheese. In a separate bowl, whisk together remaining ingredients. Pour over vegetables and mix well. Serve well chilled.

Zucchini Bean Salad

Similar to three bean salad, this can be stored in the fridge for several hours before serving to give it even more marinated flavor.

INGREDIENTS

3 small zucchini, sliced
¾ cup green pepper, chopped
½ cup onions, chopped
1 (15-oz.) can kidney beans, rinsed and drained
¼ cup oil
3 Tbsp. apple cider vinegar
1½ tsp. garlic salt
¼ tsp. pepper

SERVES 6–8

DIRECTIONS

In a large bowl, combine zucchini, green pepper, onions, and beans. In a separate bowl, whisk together oil, vinegar, salt, and pepper. Pour over vegetables and mix well. Chill.

Warm Zucchini Onion Salad

The combination of sour cream, onions, and seasoning makes this salad a deliciously different dish.

INGREDIENTS

1 cup diced onions
2 medium zucchini, coarsely grated
2 Tbsp. butter or margarine
½ tsp. Italian seasoning
¼ tsp. salt
⅛ tsp. pepper
⅓ cup sour cream (fat-free can be substituted)

SERVES
4

DIRECTIONS

Sauté onions and zucchini in butter until tender. Toss with seasonings. Stir in sour cream and heat through. Serve immediately.

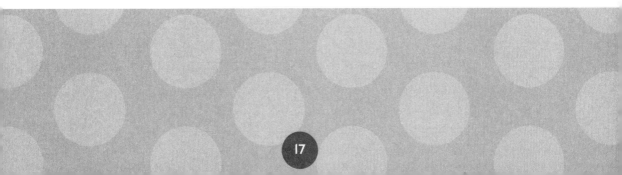

Warm Zucchini Pine Nut and Raisin Salad

Crunchy and sweet, with a minty surprise.

INGREDIENTS

2 medium zucchini, julienned
3 Tbsp. olive oil
½ cup toasted pine nuts
1 clove garlic, minced
½ cup raisins
3 Tbsp. fresh mint, finely chopped
¼ tsp. salt
¼ tsp. pepper
2 Tbsp. lemon juice

SERVES
4

DIRECTIONS

Sauté zucchini in olive oil 2 minutes until crisp tender. Reduce heat and add pine nuts, garlic, and raisins. Cook about 2 minutes. Remove from heat and stir in remaining ingredients. Serve immediately.

GETTING IN HOT WATER

In soups, stews, and chili, zucchini not only adds texture and flavor, but it also enhances the taste of what it simmers alongside.

Spicy Zucchini Potato Soup

This creamy soup has the perfect balance of flavors. I love the cilantro and jalapeños that give it such fresh, spicy warmth.

INGREDIENTS

3 Tbsp. butter or margarine
1 Tbsp. chopped jalapeño pepper with seeds
¼ tsp. fennel seeds
1 large Yukon Gold potato, peeled and cut into ½-inch cubes
4 medium zucchini, cut into ½-inch slices
1 cup chopped green onions
2½ cups chicken broth
½ cup fresh cilantro
1 tsp. fresh lime juice

SERVES
4–6

DIRECTIONS

Melt butter in heavy large saucepan over medium-high heat. Add pepper and fennel seeds; stir 30 seconds. Add potatoes, zucchini, and onions; sauté 2 minutes. Add broth and bring to boil. Reduce heat, cover, and simmer until vegetables are tender, about 15 minutes. Cool. Purée soup in batches in a blender, adding cilantro and lime juice to the first batch. Return puree to same pan. Season to taste with salt, pepper, and more lime juice, if desired. Heat and serve.

Zucchini Crab Bisque

Threads of rosy-tipped snow crabmeat look pretty atop this jade green soup.

INGREDIENTS

2 medium zucchini, cut into ½-inch slices
¼ cup fresh dill, finely chopped, plus
   several sprigs for garnish
½ pound snow crabmeat
1 tsp. kosher salt

SERVES
4

DIRECTIONS

Place zucchini, dill, and half the crabmeat in a large saucepan. Add 1¼ cups water and salt. Water will not completely cover zucchini. Bring to a rapid boil. Lower heat to medium and cover pan. Cook 20 minutes, or until zucchini is very soft. Let cool 5 minutes. Transfer contents to a blender. Blend until very smooth. Mixture should thicken and become foamy. Return to saucepan and heat until hot. Serve soup in bowls with a mound of remaining crabmeat in center of each serving. Garnish with reserved fresh dill sprigs.

Hearty Zucchini Soup

This soup is a meal in itself.

SERVES
6

INGREDIENTS

1 clove garlic, minced

3 Tbsp. olive oil

3 medium potatoes, cut into ½-inch
   cubes

1 onion, chopped

2 stalks celery, chopped

2 Tbsp. chopped fresh parsley

1 tsp. oregano

6 cups beef stock

1 large tomato, chopped

3 cups thinly sliced zucchini

2 tsp. salt

Parmesan cheese

DIRECTIONS

In a large saucepan, brown garlic in oil. Add potatoes and cook about 5 minutes. Add onion, celery, parsley, and oregano, and cook until onions are tender. Add beef stock, tomato, zucchini, and salt, and bring to boil. Reduce heat and simmer until zucchini is tender. Serve with Parmesan cheese sprinkled over the top of each serving.

Zucchini Curry and Dijon Cream Soup

A unique flavor twist, this creamy soup is so easy but tastes like you're in the finest restaurant.

INGREDIENTS

½ cup long grain rice
3 Tbsp. olive oil
6 garlic cloves, minced
3 small onions, chopped
3 Tbsp. curry
4 medium zucchini, chopped into ½-inch pieces
3 Tbsp. Dijon mustard
6 cups chicken broth
2 cups plain yogurt

SERVES
8

DIRECTIONS

Cook rice and keep warm. Heat oil and brown garlic and onions. Add curry, zucchini, and mustard. Cook until coated, about 2 minutes. Stir in broth. Bring to boil and reduce heat. Simmer covered 10 minutes. Let cool about 15 minutes. Blend until smooth. Return to saucepan. Add yogurt and rice. Heat through.

Spicy Meatball and Zucchini Soup

The salsa gives this soup its kick. This is a perfect lunch or light dinner.

INGREDIENTS

4 cups chopped zucchini
1 (28-oz.) can beef broth
2 cups salsa
2 cups water
1 Tbsp. chopped fresh cilantro
4 cups premade frozen meatballs, thawed
corn chips

SERVES
6–8

DIRECTIONS

In a large saucepan, combine zucchini, broth, salsa, and water. Bring to boil. Reduce heat and simmer 5 minutes until zucchini is slightly tender. Add meatballs and cilantro, and heat through. Serve with crushed corn chips on top.

Zucchini, Potato, and Parsley Soup

I grow green beans along with my zucchini, so this soup is always a fresh summer favorite.

INGREDIENTS

1 cup chopped onions
¼ cup olive oil
1 lb. fresh green beans, trimmed and halved
2 small zucchini cut in ½-inch cubes
2 potatoes, peeled and cubed
¾ cup chopped fresh parsley
¼ tsp. cayenne
1 (28-oz.) can Italian diced tomatoes, undrained
1 cup chicken broth
salt and pepper

SERVES 6–8

DIRECTIONS

In a large saucepan, sauté onions in olive oil until tender. Add green beans, zucchini, potatoes, parsley, and cayenne. Cook on low about 5 minutes. Add tomatoes and broth. Simmer 45 minutes. Season with salt and pepper.

Zucchini Sausage Stew

The cream corn gives this stew its hearty thickness. The Italian spices and sausage make it a savory winter favorite.

INGREDIENTS

1 lb. ground Italian sausage
2 cups celery, sliced
1 cup diced onion
3 cups quartered and sliced zucchini
2 (28-oz.) cans diced tomatoes
2 tsp. salt
1 tsp. oregano

½ tsp. basil
1 cup diced green pepper
¼ tsp. garlic powder
1 tsp. sugar
1 tsp. Italian seasoning
1 (15-oz.) can cream corn
1 (15-oz.) can butter beans, drained

SERVES
6–8

DIRECTIONS

Brown sausage and drain off fat. Add celery, onion, and zucchini, and cook about 10 minutes. Add remaining ingredients, except the corn and beans. Bring to boil, reduce heat, and simmer 30 minutes. Add corn and beans. Heat through.

Zucchini Parmesan and Rice Soup

This light and tasty soup is similar to egg drop soup, but with delightful additions.

INGREDIENTS

SERVES
8

1 medium onion, finely chopped
1 clove garlic, minced
1 Tbsp. olive oil
5 cups chicken broth
¼ cup uncooked rice

1½ cups grated zucchini
½ tsp. salt
½ tsp. pepper
1 egg (or ¼ cup egg substitute)
¼ cup grated Parmesan cheese
1 Tbsp. chopped fresh parsley

DIRECTIONS

In a large saucepan, sauté onion and garlic in oil until tender. Add broth and rice and bring to a boil. Simmer covered about 10 minutes. Add zucchini, salt, and pepper. Simmer 15 minutes until zucchini is tender. Beat together egg, cheese, and parsley. Gradually whisk into hot soup.

Zucchini Roquefort Soup

This creamy soup has a distinctive and elegant taste.

INGREDIENTS

1 small onion, chopped
1 tsp. fresh thyme, chopped, (or ½ tsp. dried)
2 Tbsp. butter or margarine
¼ cup flour
4 cups chicken broth
2 small zucchini, diced
2 oz. Roquefort cheese, crumbled
salt and pepper

**SERVES
6**

DIRECTIONS

In a large saucepan, sauté the onion and thyme in butter until tender. Add flour, and whisk while cooking for about 3 minutes. Gradually add chicken broth while continuously whisking. Bring to a boil. Add zucchini, reduce heat, and simmer covered for 45 minutes. Cool. Pour soup into blender and blend until smooth. Return to saucepan. Add cheese and serve hot. Salt and pepper to taste.

Cheesy Green Chile Zucchini Soup

My mom has made this soup for years. I love the creamy texture and the perfect mix of flavors.

INGREDIENTS

1 small onion, chopped
1 Tbsp. butter or margarine
2 cups chicken broth
2 Tbsp. chopped canned green chilies
½ tsp. salt
¼ tsp. pepper
1 (15-oz.) can cream corn

2 small zucchini, chopped
1 cup milk (skim or fat-free half-and-half can be substituted)
¼ cup flour
½ cup shredded jack cheese
½ tsp. nutmeg
chopped fresh parsley

SERVES 4–6

DIRECTIONS

In a large saucepan, sauté onion in butter until tender. Stir in broth, chilies, salt, pepper, corn, and zucchini. Heat to boiling, reduce heat, and simmer covered for 5 minutes. Stir in milk, reserving ¼ cup. Whisk ¼ cup flour into reserved milk until smooth and then add to soup. Heat until hot, but not boiling. Add cheese. Sprinkle with nutmeg and parsley.

Easy Cream Cheese Zucchini Soup

So easy, and it's a favorite with kids.

**SERVES
6**

INGREDIENTS

4 cups sliced zucchini
5 cups water
1 (8-oz.) package cream cheese (light
  cream cheese can be substituted)
1 envelope onion soup mix or vegetable soup mix

DIRECTIONS

Cook zucchini in water until tender. Pour into blender. Add cream cheese and soup mix. Blend until smooth. Return to pot and heat through.

Zucchini Bacon Soup

The bacon gives this soup a warm and smoky flavor.

INGREDIENTS

**SERVES
6**

4 slices bacon or turkey bacon, chopped
1 medium onion, chopped
1 clove garlic, minced
4 medium zucchini, cubed
2 cups beef broth
2 cups water
1 tsp. salt
¼ pepper
¼ tsp. parsley
1 Tbsp. fresh basil (or 1 tsp. dried)
grated Parmesan cheese

DIRECTIONS

In a Dutch oven, cook bacon until crisp. Drain off all fat except 1 tablespoon. Cook and stir remaining ingredients in Dutch oven, except cheese. Bring to boil. Reduce heat and simmer about 15 minutes. Put into blender and blend until smooth. Return to pot and heat through. Serve with grated cheese on top.

Zucchini Chili

Spice it up or down. This hearty chili will win over the taste testers at any chili cook-off.

INGREDIENTS

2 lbs. extra lean ground beef (or
  ground turkey)
2 cups chopped onions
6 cups chopped zucchini
4 cloves garlic, minced
2 Tbsp. oil
2 (28-oz.) cans diced tomatoes
1 (6-oz.) can tomato paste

2 (15-oz.) cans kidney beans
4 Tbsp. chili powder
1½ Tbsp. cumin
2 tsp. cayenne pepper
2 tsp. salt
water (or beer)
1 bunch cilantro, chopped

**SERVES
8**

DIRECTIONS

Brown ground beef and drain. Set aside. In a Dutch oven, sauté onions, zucchini, and garlic in oil until tender. Add tomatoes, tomato paste, beans, and spices. Add water (or beer) to bring to desired consistency. Simmer 1 hour. Serve with chopped cilantro on top.

Zucchini Festivals

Whether it's a celebration or a lampoon, cities all across the country—from Hayward, California, to Blaine County, Idaho, to Obetz, Ohio, to Ludlow, Vermont—set aside a day or two each summer to hold zucchini festivals. There are contests for the largest (some upwards of 20 pounds), the most oddly shaped, uniquely carved zukes, and even a zucchini model car race. There are games like Knock Over the Zucchini and Zuke Ring Toss as well as coloring contests and zucchini dress-up pageants.

One of the highlights of most festivals is the Zukapult, in which large, improvised catapults hurl loads of squash hundreds of feet in the air. The winner is judged on distance. Some festivals include community booths and other types of food, but all are zucchini centered, with everything from zucchini fries and burgers, to zucchini ice cream and fudge.

ALL FIRED UP

Sautéed, simmered, or fried—in the skillet, zucchini is tender, tasty, and tantalizing.

Spicy Zucchini Corn Cakes

Don't let the ease of this sizzling dish fool you! These cakes are hearty and full of flavor.

INGREDIENTS

1 (8-oz.) box cornbread mix
1 egg (or ¼ cup egg substitute)
milk
1 cup grated zucchini
¼ cup sliced green onions
salsa
sour cream (fat-free can be substituted)

SERVES
4–6

DIRECTIONS

According to directions on the box, make cornbread pancakes using the egg and enough milk for consistency. Stir in the zucchini and green onions. On a hot, greased griddle, fry pancakes until browned. Serve with salsa and sour cream.

Thai Zucchini

The zucchini and peanuts are a perfect combination with this wonderful spicy sauce.

INGREDIENTS

SERVES
4–6

2 cloves garlic, minced
1 tsp. minced fresh ginger
1 pinch dried red pepper flakes
2 tsp. olive oil
⅓ cup chopped unsalted dry roasted peanuts
3 tsp. chicken broth
3 tsp. rice vinegar
2 tsp. soy sauce
½ tsp. sugar
4 cups sliced zucchini

DIRECTIONS

In a large skillet, cook garlic, ginger, and red pepper in oil on medium high heat about 1 minute, stirring constantly. Add peanuts, broth, rice vinegar, soy sauce, and sugar. Mix well. Add zucchini, and cook about 5 minutes, stirring constantly until slightly tender.

Zucchini "Crab" Cakes

The seasoning in these cakes gives it a real seafood flavor. They are a great appetizer or light meal.

INGREDIENTS

2 cups grated zucchini
2 eggs, beaten (or ½ cup egg substitute)
1 cup seasoned bread crumbs
2 Tbsp. mayonnaise or salad dressing (fat-free can be substituted)
2 tsp. Old Bay seasoning
3 Tbsp. olive oil

SERVES 4–6

DIRECTIONS

Mix everything together. Blend well. Shape into patties. Fry in medium hot oil about 4 minutes each side. Serve with cocktail sauce or tartar sauce, if desired.

Zucchini Flats

These crispy strips of zucchini can be eaten as an appetizer or side dish. Dip in ranch dressing for even more flavor.

SERVES 4–6

INGREDIENTS

¾ cup grated Parmesan cheese
2 eggs (or ½ cup egg substitute)
2 Tbsp. flour
2 tsp. fresh parsley, chopped
¾ tsp. salt
¼ tsp. pepper

2 garlic cloves, minced
¼ cup milk (fat-free can be substituted)
2 large zucchini
⅓ cup flour
¼ cup oil
¼ cup grated Parmesan cheese

DIRECTIONS

In a shallow bowl, combine cheese, eggs, flour, parsley, salt, pepper, garlic, and milk. Whisk or beat until smooth, and then cover and refrigerate at least 15 minutes. Cut zucchini in half crosswise, then into lengthwise slices about ¼-inch thick; lightly dust each piece with flour. Heat about ¼ cup vegetable oil in a wide frying pan over medium heat; using a fork, dip each zucchini slice into cheese mixture, thickly coating both sides; place in pan, a few pieces at a time, and cook, turning once, until golden brown on both sides. Drain briefly on paper towels, and then transfer to a serving plate and keep warm until all are cooked. Sprinkle with additional Parmesan cheese.

Zucchini Jalapeño Sauté

This combination of vegetables and heat make it a great side dish for grilled meat or chicken.

INGREDIENTS

SERVES 4–6

½ cup diced onions
1 jalapeño, seeded and chopped
2 Tbsp. butter or margarine
4 cups sliced zucchini
1 large tomato, sliced
½ tsp. pepper
½ tsp. seasoning salt
1 (15¼-oz.) can corn, drained
¾ cup shredded cheddar cheese

DIRECTIONS

Sauté onions and jalapeño in butter. Add sliced zucchini and tomato. Add black pepper and seasoning salt. Cook covered 2 to 3 minutes until tender. Add corn and cover. Simmer about 7 to 10 minutes. When finished, cover with cheese on top, and sprinkle with black pepper.

Sweet and Savory Skillet Zucchini

A unique taste combination. I love this dish because it is so simple, but the flavors are a twist and add something special to the meal.

INGREDIENTS

1 large onion, sliced
6 small zucchini, sliced
3 Tbsp. butter or margarine
1 cube beef bouillon
2 Tbsp. water
1 Tbsp. brown sugar
½ tsp. seasoned salt

SERVES
6

DIRECTIONS

Sauté onion and zucchini in butter until crisp tender. Dissolve bouillon in water and add to zucchini. Cook about 15 minutes. Sprinkle brown sugar and seasoned salt over top, and turn until coated.

Sautéed Garlic Zucchini

For years this is the only way I cooked zucchini. I'm glad I now have dozens of choices, but this is still one of my favorites.

INGREDIENTS

2 cloves garlic, finely chopped
3 medium zucchini, sliced ¼-inch thick
5 Tbsp. extra virgin olive oil
1 Tbsp. lemon juice
½ tsp. salt
¼ tsp. pepper
4 Tbsp. finely chopped flat leaf parsley

SERVES 6

DIRECTIONS

Sauté garlic and zucchini in oil until browned. Sprinkle with lemon juice, salt, and pepper, and cook for a couple minutes. Sprinkle with parsley and cook 1 minute. Serve immediately.

Zucchini Alfredo

A low-fat and vitamin-packed way to enjoy an Italian favorite. As the zucchini strips cook, they become tender and the texture is similar to noodles.

INGREDIENTS

SERVES 6

3 medium zucchini
2 Tbsp. olive oil
½ Tbsp. grated Parmesan cheese
½ cup sour cream (fat-free or light can be substituted)

DIRECTIONS

Slice zucchini into evenly sized juliennedd strips. Sauté in oil until tender. Mix together cheese and sour cream. Stir into zucchini and heat through.

Loaded Zucchini Sauté

With all the makings of a loaded baked potato, this dish is a great side for steaks or ribs.

INGREDIENTS

2 slices bacon or turkey bacon, diced
2 medium zucchini, sliced
1 tsp. basil
¼ tsp. salt
¼ tsp. pepper
¼ cup shredded cheddar cheese
1 Tbsp. grated Parmesan cheese
1 green onion, chopped
sour cream (fat-free can be substituted)

SERVES
4

DIRECTIONS

Fry bacon until crisp. Drain on paper towel. Remove all but 1 tablespoon of grease in pan. Add zucchini, basil, salt, and pepper to pan. Sauté until tender. Add bacon and cheeses, and heat until melted. Sprinkle green onion on top, and serve with sour cream.

Zucchini Fries

Kids can't resist these crunchy and flavorful fries!

INGREDIENTS

1 medium zucchini
½ cup flour
1 tsp. onion salt
1 tsp. dried oregano
¼ tsp. garlic powder
1 egg, beaten (or ¼ cup egg substitute)
⅓ cup milk (fat-free can be substituted)
2 tsp. oil
4 cups crushed corn Chex cereal
oil for deep-frying

SERVES 4

DIRECTIONS

Cut zucchini in half widthwise, and then cut each half lengthwise into 8 wedges. Set aside. In one bowl, combine flour, onion salt, oregano, and garlic powder. In another bowl, combine the egg, milk, and oil; stir into the dry ingredients just until blended. Dip zucchini wedges in batter, and then roll in crushed cereal. In a deep fryer or electric fry pan, heat oil to 375 degrees. Fry zucchini wedges, a few at a time, for 3 to 4 minutes or until golden brown. Drain on paper towels.

Zucchini Crisps

The lemon juice gives these crispy treats a little kick.

INGREDIENTS

SERVES 6

3 medium zucchini
salt
pepper
flour
1 egg, beaten (or ¼ cup egg substitute)
1 Tbsp. milk
1 cup fine cracker crumbs
3 Tbsp. butter, oil, or stick margarine
lemon juice

DIRECTIONS

Wash and slice off ends of zucchini. Cut lengthwise into ½-inch sticks. Sprinkle with salt and pepper, and roll in flour. Combine egg and milk. Dip sticks in mixture and roll in crumbs. Fry in hot butter or oil until crisp on all sides, about 5 minutes. Sprinkle with lemon juice.

Zucchini Fritters

Crispy on the outside and tender on the inside, these fritters are a great lunch, snack, or appetizer.

INGREDIENTS

salt
2 medium zucchini, coarsely grated
¼ tsp. pepper
1 egg, beaten (or ¼ cup egg substitute)
2 green onions, finely chopped
½ cup flour
½ cup olive oil
sour cream (fat-free can be substituted)

**SERVES
4**

DIRECTIONS

Salt the zucchini and put in a colander to drain. Try to remove as much moisture as possible using paper towels. In a large bowl, mix together zucchini, pepper, egg, onions, and flour. Drop by large spoonfuls (about 2 tablespoons each) into hot oil in large skillet. Flatten slightly. Cook, turning once until browned, about 5 minutes on each side. Drain on paper towels. Sprinkle with salt and serve with sour cream.

Zucchini and Thyme

Such a simple recipe, but such a unique and wonderful taste.

INGREDIENTS

2 cups zucchini, coarsely grated
2 Tbsp. olive oil
1 Tbsp. thyme

SERVES
4–6

DIRECTIONS

Let the zucchini sit in a colander to drain excess juice. Use a paper towel to get any extra moisture. Sauté zucchini sprinkled with thyme in olive oil until crisp tender.

Zucchini Mushroom Pasta

Both zucchini and mushrooms release flavorful juices when cooked. This makes for a wonderful sauce for pasta. This is a great side dish or a light lunch.

INGREDIENTS

1 medium zucchini, sliced thin
1 cup sliced mushrooms
1 garlic clove, minced
1 Tbsp. olive oil
½ pound spaghetti or penne pasta,
    cooked and drained
½ cup grated Parmesan cheese

SERVES 4–6

DIRECTIONS

Sauté zucchini, mushrooms, and garlic in olive oil until tender. Sprinkle with salt. Add pasta and cheese, and let simmer 3 minutes in juices. Toss to mix well.

Parmesan, Peas, and Zucchini Pasta

I love this dish for lunch on a cold day. It's creamy and hearty, but with a fresh taste because of the basil.

INGREDIENTS

SERVES 4

1 cup fresh or frozen peas
2 medium zucchini, cut into strips about ½-inch thick
olive oil
1 cup coarsely chopped fresh basil
1 pound spaghetti, cooked and drained
1 cup plain yogurt or sour cream (fat-free can be substituted)
salt
pepper
½ cup grated Parmesan cheese

DIRECTIONS

Cook peas in boiling salted water about 4 minutes. Drain. In a large skillet, sauté zucchini in olive oil until tender. Add basil and peas, and cook about 2 minutes. Add spaghetti and yogurt or sour cream, and cook until heated through. Sprinkle with salt, pepper, and Parmesan cheese. Toss well.

Zucchini Tempura

These are wonderful with dipping sauces. I like ranch dressing best.

INGREDIENTS

**SERVES
4–6**

¾ cup cornstarch
¼ cup flour
1 tsp. baking powder
½ tsp. salt
¼ tsp. pepper
½ cup water
1 tsp. soy sauce
1 egg, beaten (or ¼ cup egg substitute)
vegetable oil
4 cups sliced zucchini

DIRECTIONS

Mix the cornstarch, flour, baking powder, salt, and pepper. Add water, soy sauce, and egg, and whisk together until smooth. In a large skillet, heat ½-inch deep oil over medium high heat. Dip zucchini slices in batter mixture and fry in oil for about 2 to 3 minutes, turning once. Drain on paper towels.

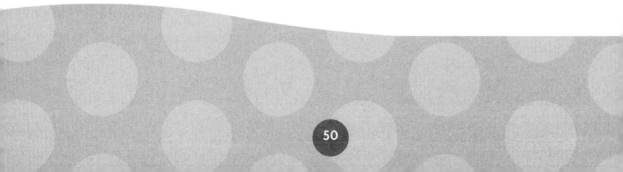

Grilled Marinated Zucchini

When firing up the grill, make room for these savory slices. They cook about the same amount of time as a medium rare steak!

INGREDIENTS

2 large zucchini, cut lengthwise into ½-inch slices
extra virgin olive oil
balsamic vinegar
garlic salt
lemon pepper

SERVES
4–6

DIRECTIONS

Place zucchini slices in a gallon-size ziplock plastic bag. Mix oil and vinegar, and pour over zucchini. Close the bag and shake to coat. Marinate about 30 minutes. Grill zucchini about 4 minutes on each side or until tender. Sprinkle with garlic salt or lemon pepper to taste.

Zucchini Spaghetti

This is a simple and tasty alternative to pasta, but no carbs are in these "noodles."

INGREDIENTS

2 medium zucchini, very coarsely grated into thin strips
1 tsp. garlic salt
2 Tbsp. butter or margarine
bottled spaghetti sauce
Parmesan cheese

SERVES
4

DIRECTIONS

Sprinkle zucchini strips with garlic salt and sauté in butter until tender. Serve with heated spaghetti sauce and Parmesan cheese.

Cheesy Zucchini Flapjacks

This unique and tasty side dish is a great substitute for potatoes or rice.

INGREDIENTS

2 cups grated zucchini
¼ cup shredded cheddar cheese
⅓ cup biscuit mix (reduced fat version works great)
2 eggs, beaten (or ½ cup egg substitute)
4 green onions, chopped
¼ cup green pepper, chopped
½ tsp. salt
¼ tsp. pepper
¼ tsp. garlic powder

SERVES 4–6

DIRECTIONS

Mix together all ingredients. Mixture will be thick. Shape into pancakes and fry in oil about 4 minutes on each side. Drain on paper towels.

Spicy Zucchini Skillet Medley

Ready in minutes, this wonderful vegetable dish has some extra zip.

INGREDIENTS

5 cups zucchini, thinly sliced
4 ripe plum tomatoes, seeded and chopped
1 onion, chopped
½ cup chopped fresh cilantro
¼ cup chopped fresh parsley
2 cloves garlic, minced
3 jalapeños, seeded and chopped
1¼ cups white wine (or white wine vinegar)
1 cup water
¼ cup sliced black olives
2 cups shredded Jack cheese
½ tsp. salt
½ tsp. pepper

SERVES 6–8

DIRECTIONS

In a large skillet combine zucchini, tomatoes, onions, cilantro, parsley, garlic, jalapeños, wine (or vinegar), and water. Cook over medium heat for about 15 minutes until zucchini is crisp tender. Stir in olives, cheese, salt, and pepper. Cook until cheese melts. Serve immediately.

Escape Artists

It is not uncommon, while carefully spreading the large, prickly leaves of your overcrowded zucchini plants, to discover a behemoth that somehow escaped your previous searches and was given the chance to explode in size. Every year I find some of these monsters. But one year, when the snow came early and I was unable to finish my final harvest and subsequent tilling before the frost, I found that many of these zucchini giants had eluded me.

When the chill had killed the annuals and sent the other plants and trees into their winter dormancy, I stood at my kitchen window and stared out at the fenced-off garden. There, in the glistening untouched snow, lay almost a dozen dark green mounds. Those sneaky zukes had managed to escape my searches and elude my kitchen and now were caught by old man winter. It was a zucchini graveyard of sorts. But it was also a comforting reminder of what I had to look forward to, come spring.

OVEN LOVIN'

Zucchini plays well with others in casseroles, quiches, and bakes

Mexican Zucchini Breakfast Casserole

This dish may clear your sinuses. If you want a milder taste, substitute regular jack or cheddar cheese and use canned green chilies instead of jalapeños.

INGREDIENTS

4 cups zucchini, quartered and sliced
oil
1 small onion, chopped
3 jalapeños, seeded and cut into strips
3 eggs, beaten (or ¾ cup egg substitute)
½ cup self-rising flour
1 cup shredded pepper jack cheese
½ tsp. cayenne pepper
1 tsp. salt

SERVES
4–6

DIRECTIONS

Sauté zucchini in oil and cook until tender and beginning to brown. Using a slotted spoon, transfer them to a large bowl. In the same skillet, add onion and jalapeño strips, reserving some for the garnish. Fry until tender. Using a slotted spoon, add onions and jalapeños to the bowl with the zucchini. Beat eggs in another bowl. Add flour, cheese, and pepper. Mix well. Stir into zucchini mixture along with the salt. Pour into a buttered 9-inch round dish. Bake at 350 degrees for 30 minutes until firm to the touch and golden. Allow to cool. Serve zucchini in thick wedges, garnished with remaining jalapeño strips.

Zucchini Crab Casserole

I love crab, so this dish combines two of my favorites into one incredible meal.

INGREDIENTS

3–5 medium zucchini, cut into ½-inch slices
1½ cups biscuit mix
1½ cups shredded sharp American cheese
1 cup onions, chopped
1 cup or 1 (6½ -oz.) can of crabmeat, drained
½ cup oil
3 eggs (or ¾ cup egg substitute)
1 tsp. dried oregano
1 tsp. salt
½ tsp. pepper

SERVES 6–8

DIRECTIONS

Mix all ingredients together and spread into a greased 9x13 baking dish. Bake, uncovered, at 450 degrees for 30 minutes or until golden brown and a knife inserted comes out clean.

Zucchini Crescent Pie

I was told a recipe similar to this one was awarded a $40,000 prize in the Pillsbury bake-off! The crust is light and flaky, making this a wonderful brunch dish.

INGREDIENTS

SERVES 8

4 cups zucchini, thinly sliced
1 cup onion, chopped
1 glove garlic, chopped
¼ cup butter or margarine
½ cup chopped fresh parsley
½ tsp. garlic salt
½ tsp. pepper
½ tsp. Italian seasoning
2 eggs, beaten (or ½ cup egg substitute)
2 cups shredded mozzarella cheese
1 (8 oz.) can of refrigerated crescent rolls (reduced fat version works great)
2 tsp. Dijon mustard

DIRECTIONS

In a 10-inch skillet, cook zucchini, onions, and garlic in butter until tender. Add parsley and seasonings. In a large bowl, blend eggs and cheese. Add vegetable mixture. Separate crescent-roll dough into 8 triangles; place in an ungreased 10-inch pie plate or 8x12 baking dish. Press dough over bottom and up sides to form crust; spread crust with mustard. Pour vegetable mixture evenly into crust and bake at 375 degrees for 18–20 minutes, or until knife inserted comes out clean. Let cool 10 minutes before serving.

Creamy Zucchini Chicken Casserole

Talk about comfort food. This dish is perfect on days you want to curl up and stay indoors.

INGREDIENTS

SERVES 6–8

2 cups grated zucchini

6 cups cooked and diced chicken

2 (10.5-oz.) cans cream of chicken soup (fat-free can be substituted)

¾ cup milk (fat-free can be substituted)

¾ cup mayonnaise or salad dressing (fat-free can be substituted)

2–3 Tbsp. lemon juice

1 cup shredded cheddar cheese

½ cup butter or stick margarine

¾ cup dried bread crumbs

DIRECTIONS

Spray a 9 x 13 baking dish with cooking spray. Cover bottom with the zucchini. Cover zucchini with chicken pieces. In a mixing bowl combine soup, milk, mayo, lemon juice, and cheese. Pour this mixture over the chicken. Melt butter and stir in bread crumbs. Sprinkle this over the top of the casserole. Bake at 350 degrees 25 minutes or until bread crumbs are toasted and liquid is bubbling.

Parmesan Sausage Zucchini Boats

These are so rich and flavorful, and the presentation is perfect!

INGREDIENTS

4 medium zucchini
1 pound bulk sausage
1 small onion, chopped
1 clove garlic, minced
⅔ cup seasoned bread crumbs
½ cup plus 2 Tbsp. grated
  Parmesan cheese

1 egg, beaten (or ¼ cup egg
  substitute)
¼ tsp. salt
½ cup water

**SERVES
8**

DIRECTIONS

Cut zucchini lengthwise. Scoop out seeds and discard. Scoop out pulp, leaving a ¼-inch shell. Chop pulp. In a large skillet, brown sausage. Add onion, garlic, and chopped zucchini pulp. Sauté 5 minutes. Remove from heat. Add bread crumbs, ½ cup cheese, and egg. Mix well. Sprinkle salt in each zucchini shell. Fill evenly with meat and zucchini mixture. Sprinkle with remaining Parmesan cheese. Place shells in ungreased baking dishes. Pour ½ cup water into bottom of each dish. Cover with foil. Bake at 350 degrees for 15 minutes. Uncover and bake another 15 minutes or until zucchini is tender.

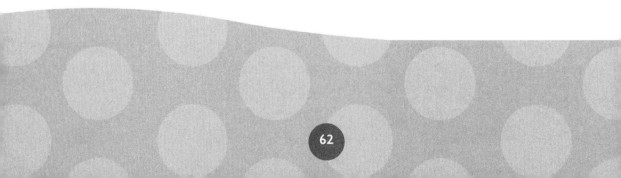

Zucchini Cheese Chips

These are baked, not fried, and the Parmesan cheese gives them an added touch.

INGREDIENTS

SERVES
4

¼ cup fine dry bread crumbs
¼ cup grated Parmesan cheese
¼ tsp. seasoned salt
¼ tsp. garlic powder
⅛ tsp. pepper
2½ cups thinly sliced zucchini
2 Tbsp. milk (fat-free can be substituted)

DIRECTIONS

Combine bread crumbs, cheese, salt, garlic powder, and pepper. Dip zucchini slices in milk and then in bread crumb mixture. Place on greased wire rack on a baking sheet. Bake at 425 degrees for 30 minutes or until crisp and lightly browned.

Zucchini Meatloaf

This meatloaf is so moist but without all the fat!

INGREDIENTS

2 eggs, beaten (or ½ cup egg
  substitute)
2 cups grated zucchini
⅓ cup seasoned bread crumbs
⅓ cup chopped onion
1 tsp. salt
½ tsp. oregano

¼ tsp. salt
1½ lbs. extra lean ground beef

Topping:
1 Tbsp. brown sugar
2 Tbsp. ketchup
½ tsp. yellow mustard

SERVES
8

DIRECTIONS

In a large bowl, mix all ingredients until well blended. Press mixture into ungreased 9½-inch deep-dish glass pie plate. Bake at 350 degrees for 35 minutes. Meanwhile, in a small bowl, mix all topping ingredients. Remove meatloaf from oven; pour off drippings. Spread topping over loaf. Return to oven; bake 10 to 15 minutes longer or until thoroughly cooked in center and meat thermometer reads 160. Let stand 5 minutes before serving for juices to set up.

Zucchini Hamburger Pie

This layered dish is satisfying and tasty. It's great served with mashed potatoes.

INGREDIENTS

pie crust
½ lb. extra lean ground beef
1 small onion, chopped
½ cup green pepper, chopped
1 tsp. fresh parsley, chopped
½ tsp. garlic salt
1 tsp. oregano

½ cup dried bread crumbs
¼ cup grated Parmesan
    cheese
4 medium zucchini, sliced
1 (8-oz.) can sliced
    tomatoes, undrained

SERVES 6–8

DIRECTIONS

Line a 9-inch pie shell with crust. Brown ground beef, onion, pepper, parsley, and spices. Drain fat. Stir in bread crumbs and cheese. Mix well. Alternate ground beef mixture with zucchini slices, and then top with tomato slices. Pour juice from tomatoes over entire pie. Top with another crust and seal edges. Put several slits in top crust. Bake at 350 degrees for 40–45 minutes. Put foil over top if it browns too quickly.

Zucchini Ham and Dill Pie

Definitely different, but this combination of flavors is a favorite.

SERVES 6

INGREDIENTS

1 pie crust
1 large onion, sliced thin
3 small zucchini, sliced
1 clove garlic, minced
2 Tbsp. olive oil
2 cups cubed ham
1 cup shredded Swiss cheese
1¼ cups sour cream (or fat-free sour cream)

1 tsp. dill weed
1 tsp. salt
¼ tsp. pepper
2 Tbsp. butter or stick margarine, melted
1½ cups bread crumbs
¼ cup grated Parmesan cheese

DIRECTIONS

Line a 9-inch pie plate with crust. Bake at 350 degrees for 10 minutes. Sauté onion, zucchini, and garlic in olive oil approximately 5 minutes or until tender but not soft. Remove from heat. Mix together ham, Swiss cheese, sour cream, dill weed, salt, and pepper. Spoon mixture into pie shell. Mix melted butter, bread crumbs, and Parmesan cheese together, and sprinkle on top. Bake at 350 degrees for 35 minutes. Let stand 10 minutes before serving.

Artichoke Zucchini Quiche

This crustless quiche is perfect for a potluck. The artichokes give it a distinct flavor.

INGREDIENTS

4 eggs, beaten (or 1 cup egg substitute)
½ cup oil
3 cups grated zucchini
2 cloves garlic, crushed
1 (15-oz.) can artichoke hearts, drained and chopped
½ cup grated Parmesan cheese
1 cup biscuit mix
½ tsp. salt
½ tsp. pepper
½ tsp. oregano

SERVES 6–8

DIRECTIONS

Mix together eggs, oil, zucchini, garlic, and artichoke hearts. In a separate bowl mix together cheese, biscuit mix, and spices. Add to zucchini mixture and blend well. Pour into a greased 9-inch pie plate. Bake at 350 degrees for about 40 minutes or until knife comes out clean. Serve warm.

Zucchini Beef Casserole

The rice and beef make this a hearty dinner, and the cottage cheese makes it moist and delicious.

INGREDIENTS

1 lb. extra lean ground beef
1 cup onions, chopped
2 cloves garlic, minced
1 tsp. basil
½ tsp. salt
½ tsp. oregano
½ tsp. pepper
2 cups cooked rice
1 cup tomato sauce

4 cups sliced zucchini
1 Tbsp. olive oil
1 cup cottage cheese (fat-free works fine)
2 eggs, beaten (or ½ cup egg substitute)
1 cup shredded mozzarella cheese
Parmesan cheese

DIRECTIONS

Brown ground beef, onions, and garlic. Drain and remove to large mixing bowl. Mix in spices, rice, and tomato sauce. Sauté zucchini in oil until tender. Put half of zucchini mixture evenly in the bottom of a large greased casserole dish. Spread beef mixture over top. In a bowl, mix together cottage cheese and eggs. Spread over beef mixture. Top with remaining zucchini. Spread mozzarella cheese over top. Bake at 350 degrees for 30 minutes. Serve with Parmesan cheese sprinkled on top.

Zucchini Enchiladas

A unique variation on a traditional Mexican dish.

INGREDIENTS

2 zucchini
1 small onion
½ green pepper, seeded
1 clove garlic, minced
1 Tbsp. olive oil
⅛ tsp. chili powder
4 flour tortillas
1 (15-oz.) can enchilada sauce
1 cup shredded cheddar cheese

SERVES
4

DIRECTIONS

Slice zucchini thinly in lengthwise strips. Slice onion and green pepper into thin strips. Sauté zucchini, onions, peppers, and garlic in olive oil until tender. Toss with chili powder. Divide zucchini mixture onto tortillas. Sprinkle each with about 2 tablespoons of cheese and roll up. Spread ½ cup enchilada sauce on bottom of 8x8 baking dish. Place rolled enchiladas on top. Cover with remaining sauce. Sprinkle remaining cheese evenly over top. Bake at 350 degrees for 20 minutes.

Zucchini Caruso

My grandmother made this dish when I was a child. It is creamy but spicy and is still one of my favorites. It satisfies even my brother's big appetite!

INGREDIENTS

½ pound mild Italian sausage
½ cup chopped onion
1 clove garlic, crushed
2 Tbsp. butter or stick margarine
2 Tbsp. flour
½ tsp. Italian seasoning
⅛ tsp. salt

⅛ tsp. pepper
1 cup milk
1½ cups shredded
  mozzarella cheese
2 cups cooked noodles
½ cup halved and sliced zucchini
½ cup chopped tomatoes

SERVES 6

DIRECTIONS

Brown sausage, onion, and garlic until sausage is cooked and crumbled. Drain and set aside. Melt butter. Stir in flour and seasonings until smooth. Remove from heat and whisk in milk. Bring to boil, stirring constantly 1 minute. Reduce heat to low. Stir in ¾ cup of the cheese. Add sausage mixture, noodles, zucchini, and tomatoes. Place in buttered 1 quart casserole dish. Bake at 350 degrees for 30 minutes. Sprinkle with remaining cheese. Return to oven just until cheese melts.

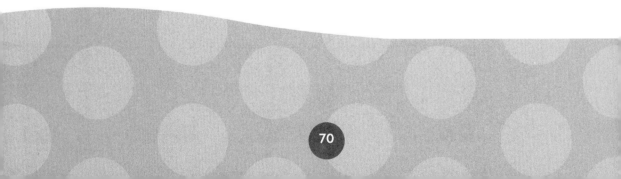

Cottage and Corn Stuffed Zucchini

This is something I love to serve to guests. The presentation is unique, and the taste is light. It's perfect as a side dish for just about anything.

INGREDIENTS

6 zucchini
1 cup canned corn, drained
½ cup cottage cheese (fat-free works fine)
⅛ tsp. salt
⅛ tsp. pepper
2 Tbsp. green onions, chopped
¼ cup grated Parmesan cheese

SERVES
6

DIRECTIONS

Cut zucchini in half lengthwise and scoop out seeds. Mix together corn, cottage cheese, salt, pepper, and green onions. Spoon mixture into zucchini so that they are mounded on top. Sprinkle with Parmesan cheese. Place zucchini in greased baking dish. Bake at 350 degrees for 20 minutes or until zucchini is tender and cheese has melted.

Zucchini Bacon and Rice Casserole

A complete dinner that is a tasty combination of hearty favorites and fresh herbs.

**SERVES
6**

INGREDIENTS

4 slices bacon or turkey bacon, chopped

4 cups zucchini, diced

1 onion, chopped

2 cloves garlic, minced

2 cups cooked rice

1 tsp. tarragon

1 Tbsp. chopped fresh basil

2 Tbsp. chopped fresh parsley

¼ tsp. salt

¼ tsp. pepper

¼ cup grated Parmesan cheese

½ cup shredded cheddar cheese

DIRECTIONS

Cook bacon until almost crisp. Add zucchini, onion, and garlic, and sauté until tender. Stir in rice, seasonings, and Parmesan cheese. Place in 8x12 baking dish. Sprinkle with cheddar cheese. Bake at 350 degrees for 20 minutes or until cheese is melted.

Zucchini Pizza Quiche

Kids can't resist this wonderfully tasty quiche, and without a crust it can be made in a matter of minutes.

INGREDIENTS

2 eggs, beaten (or ½ cup egg substitute)
¼ cup flour
1 tsp. olive oil
2 cups grated zucchini
1 cup shredded mozzarella cheese
1 cup grated Parmesan cheese
¼ cup pepperoni slices
½ tsp. basil
¼ tsp. oregano

SERVES
4–6

DIRECTIONS

Whisk together eggs, flour, and oil until smooth. Add zucchini, ½ cup mozzarella, and ½ cup Parmesan cheese. Blend well. Place in a greased 10-inch pie plate. Bake at 350 degrees for 30 minutes. Remove from oven. Sprinkle with remaining mozzarella and Parmesan cheese. Lay slices of pepperoni evenly over top. Sprinkle with basil and oregano. Bake another 10 minutes or until cheese melts.

Zucchini Garden Casserole

I love the loads of vegetables in this cheesy dish. The breadcrumb topping gives it a homey finish.

SERVES 6–8

INGREDIENTS

3 zucchini, quartered and sliced

3 yellow squash, quartered and sliced

1 large onion, chopped

1 green pepper, seeded and chopped

1 cup sliced mushrooms

3 Tbsp. butter or stick margarine

2 large tomatoes, chopped

3 Tbsp. flour

3 Tbsp. sugar

2 cups shredded cheddar cheese

1 cup seasoned bread crumbs

¼ cup butter or stick margarine

DIRECTIONS

Sauté zucchini, yellow squash, onion, pepper, and mushrooms in butter until tender. Add tomatoes, flour, and sugar. Cook and stir about 3 minutes until it starts to thicken. Pour into a greased 9x13 baking dish. Spread cheese evenly over top. Sprinkle with bread crumbs and dot with butter. Bake at 350 degrees for 20 minutes until bubbly and cheese has melted.

Zucchini Italian Bake

This oven pie is full of Italian flavor and can be doubled for a potluck or buffet.

INGREDIENTS

1½ cups biscuit mix (low fat works fine)
½ cup oil
4 eggs, beaten (or 1 cup egg substitute)
½ cup grated Romano cheese
3 cups grated zucchini
1½ cups onion, chopped
½ cup chopped green pepper
1 clove garlic, minced
2 Tbsp. chopped fresh parsley
¼ tsp. salt
2 cups diced pepperoni
½ cup sliced mushrooms

SERVES
6–8

DIRECTIONS

Mix together biscuit mix, oil, eggs, and cheese. Blend well. Add in other ingredients, mixing well after each. Pour into a greased 9x13 baking dish. Bake at 350 degrees for 1 hour.

Creamy Zucchini Stuffing Casserole

This decadent casserole is a combination of tastes that is smooth and satisfying.

INGREDIENTS

SERVES
4–6

3 cups zucchini, chopped
½ cup onions, chopped
2 Tbsp. butter or stick margarine
1 (8-oz.) box stuffing mix
1 cup sour cream (fat-free works fine)
1 (10.5-oz.) can cream of chicken soup

DIRECTIONS

Fry zucchini and onions in butter just until tender. In a bowl, mix together stuffing and seasoning packet (included in the box), sour cream, and soup. Stir in zucchini and onions. Place in a lightly greased 8x8 baking dish. Bake at 350 degrees for 30 minutes.

Mashed Zucchini Mushroom Casserole

So smooth and tasty, this dish is perfect for a light dinner or a hearty side dish.

INGREDIENTS

1 onion, chopped
2 cloves garlic, chopped
1 cup sliced mushrooms
2 Tbsp. olive oil
6 cups steamed and mashed zucchini
3 eggs, beaten (or ¾ cup egg substitute)
¼ cup seasoned bread crumbs
1½ cups shredded jack cheese
½ tsp. salt
½ tsp. pepper

SERVES
6–8

DIRECTIONS

Sauté onion, garlic, and mushrooms in oil until tender. Mix in mashed zucchini. In a separate bowl stir together eggs, bread crumbs, cheese, salt, and pepper. Stir in zucchini mixture and blend well. Pour into a greased 9x13 baking dish. Bake at 350 degrees for 40 minutes.

Mexican Zucchini Corn Casserole

Spicy, but creamy. I like the combination of sour cream and green chilies. And the chips give it a great crunch.

INGREDIENTS

SERVES
4–6

3 cups sliced zucchini
1 cup canned corn, drained
2 cups tomato sauce
1½ tsp. chili powder
¼ tsp. cayenne pepper
¼ tsp. cumin
1 tsp. apple cider vinegar

2 cups slightly crushed tortilla
  chips
1 (4-oz.) can diced green chilies
1½ cups shredded cheddar cheese
¾ cup sour cream (fat-free can be
  substituted)
2 green onions, chopped

DIRECTIONS

Steam zucchini until tender. Mix together zucchini, corn, tomato sauce, spices, vinegar, chips, and chilies. Pour into greased 8x8 baking dish. Bake at 350 degrees for 15 minutes. Remove from oven. Put cheese evenly over top. Bake an additional 10 minutes or until cheese is melted. Serve with a dollop of sour cream, and sprinkle with green onions.

Zucchini Jack Casserole

Green chilies and jack cheese are always a great combination. This casserole is perfect for an outdoor buffet or summer brunch.

INGREDIENTS

3 Tbsp. flour
2 tsp. baking powder
½ tsp. salt
4 eggs, beaten (or 1 cup egg substitute)
½ cup milk (fat-free works fine)
4 cups sliced zucchini
3 cups shredded jack cheese
1 small onion, chopped
1 (4-oz.) can diced green chilies
¼ cup chopped fresh parsley
1 clove garlic, minced
1 cup seasoned croutons
3 Tbsp. butter or margarine, melted

**SERVES
6–8**

DIRECTIONS

Whisk together flour, baking powder, salt, eggs, and milk until smooth. Stir in zucchini, cheese, onion, chilies, parsley, and garlic. Pour into a greased 9 x 13 baking dish. Toss croutons in butter and sprinkle over top. Bake at 350 degrees for about 40 minutes or until set.

Layered Zucchini Tomato Casserole

Zucchini and tomatoes complement each other perfectly. This dish is a perfect way to serve your garden-fresh bounty.

INGREDIENTS

SERVES 6–8

1 cup shredded cheddar cheese
⅓ cup grated Parmesan cheese
1 clove garlic, minced
1 tsp. oregano
1 tsp. basil
½ tsp. salt

¼ tsp. pepper
5 cups sliced zucchini
2 large tomatoes, sliced
⅛ cup onions, chopped
¼ cup butter or stick margarine
½ cup dry bread crumbs

DIRECTIONS

Combine cheeses, garlic, and seasonings in a bowl. In a buttered 8 x 12 baking dish, arrange half the zucchini in an even layer. Sprinkle with a quarter of the cheese and spice mixture. Arrange half the tomatoes in an even layer on top. Sprinkle again with a quarter of the cheese mixture. Continue another layer with the other half of the zucchini, a quarter of the cheese mixture, and the other half of the tomatoes. Sprinkle the last quarter cup of cheese mixture on top. In a skillet, sauté onions in butter until soft. Add bread crumbs and stir until coated. Spread this mixture on top. Cover loosely with foil and bake at 375 degrees for 30 minutes. Uncover and continue baking for 20 minutes or until bread crumbs are browned and zucchini is tender.

Zucchini Corn Casserole

This light and tasty dish combines two hearty vegetables in a fluffy filling.

INGREDIENTS

6 small zucchini, stems removed
1 (15-oz.) can cream style corn
4 eggs, beaten (or 1 cup egg substitute)
1 medium onion, chopped
1 small green pepper, seeded and chopped
2 Tbsp. butter or stick margarine, melted
1¼ tsp. salt
¼ tsp. pepper
1 cup shredded cheddar cheese
paprika

**SERVES
8–10**

DIRECTIONS

Cook zucchini in boiling salted water until crisp tender, about 6 minutes. Drain and cut into chunks. Mix zucchini with corn and eggs. Sauté onion and pepper in butter until tender, about 5 minutes. Add to zucchini mixture with salt and pepper. Mix well and place in a greased 2-quart casserole dish. Sprinkle cheese on top and sprinkle with a little paprika. Bake at 350 degrees for 40 minutes.

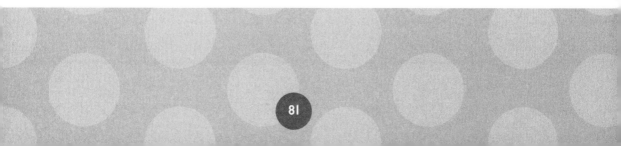

Zucchini Ratatouille

This version of the French stew is baked. It is best if you let it sit for a while before serving so the juices can set.

INGREDIENTS

2 large onions, sliced
2 cloves garlic, minced
1 medium eggplant, cut into 1-inch cubes
6 medium zucchini, thickly sliced
1 green bell pepper, seeded and cut into chunks
1 red bell pepper, seeded and cut into chunks
4 large tomatoes, cut into chunks

2 tsp. salt
1 tsp. basil
½ cup finely chopped fresh parsley
4 Tbsp. olive oil
fresh parsley
tomato slices

**SERVES
8–10**

DIRECTIONS

Layer onions, garlic, eggplant, zucchini, peppers, and tomatoes in a 6-quart casserole dish. Sprinkle with salt, basil, and parsley in between each layer. Drizzle top layer with olive oil. Cover casserole and bake at 350 degrees for 2 hours. Occasionally baste casserole with liquid from vegetables. Uncover and bake another hour. Remove from oven and stir gently. Let it sit for about 30 minutes. Garnish with fresh parsley and tomato slices.

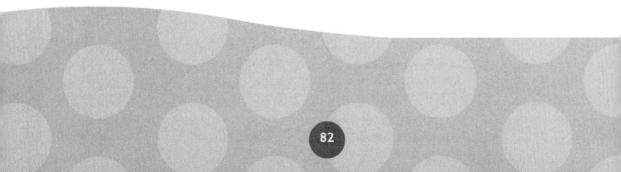

Zucchini Mushroom Rice Bake

Creamy and cheesy, with a smoky hint of bacon.

INGREDIENTS

4 medium zucchini, sliced thin
¾ cup shredded cheddar cheese
½ cup uncooked long grain rice
1 (10.5-oz.) can cream of mushroom soup
1 cup water
1 (3–4-oz.) can sliced mushrooms, undrained
1 tsp. salt
¼ tsp. pepper
2 slices bacon or turkey bacon, cut into 1-inch pieces

SERVES
4–6

DIRECTIONS

Arrange a third of the zucchini in the bottom of a well-buttered 2-quart casserole dish. Top with a third of the cheese and half of the rice. Make another layer of a third zucchini, a third of the cheese, and remaining rice. Top with remaining zucchini. In a saucepan, combine soup, water, mushrooms (including liquid), salt, and pepper. Heat and pour over vegetables in dish. Sprinkle with remaining cheese. Arrange bacon pieces on top. Cover and bake at 350 degrees for 25 minutes. Uncover and bake another 20 minutes.

Zucchini Parmesan Cheese Bake

Hearty and with a hint of Italian flavor, this dish is great for brunch or a light lunch.

INGREDIENTS

3 cups quartered and sliced zucchini
1 small onion, chopped
1 cup biscuit mix (low fat works fine)
½ cup grated Parmesan cheese
¼ tsp. basil
½ tsp. oregano
salt and pepper
½ tsp. garlic powder
4 eggs, beaten (or 1 cup egg substitute)
½ cup olive oil

SERVES
8

DIRECTIONS

Mix zucchini, onion, biscuit mix, cheese, basil, oregano, salt, pepper, and garlic powder. Combine oil and eggs. Add to zucchini mix, turning until zucchini mix is evenly coated. Pour into a buttered 9-inch pie plate. Bake at 350 degrees for 30 minutes or until golden. Test by placing a butter knife in the center, and if it comes out clean, it is done.

Cheddar Stuffed Zucchini

This cheesy dish is not only delicious as a side dish, but also perfect for a light lunch.

INGREDIENTS

3 medium zucchini
1½ cups soft bread crumbs
½ cup shredded cheddar cheese
¼ cup minced onions
1¼ tsp. salt
¼ tsp. pepper
2 eggs, beaten (or ½ cup egg substitute)
2 Tbsp. minced fresh parsley
2 Tbsp. butter or stick margarine, cut in small cubes
¼ cup shredded cheddar cheese

**SERVES
6–8**

DIRECTIONS

Boil zucchini in salted water for 5 minutes. Remove ends and cut in half lengthwise. Remove flesh, leaving ¼-inch for shell. Chop flesh and mix in a large bowl with bread crumbs, cheese, onions, salt, pepper, eggs, and parsley. Divide and spoon mixture into zucchini shells. Arrange in buttered baking dish. Sprinkle with cheese. Bake at 350 degrees for 30 minutes.

Ritzy Zucchini

Rich and cheesy, this dish is extra special with a buttery rich crumble topping.

INGREDIENTS

2 medium zucchini, grated
1 onion, chopped
1 (16-oz.) box round butter crackers, crushed
4 Tbsp. butter or stick margarine, melted
1 cup shredded cheddar cheese

SERVES
4–6

DIRECTIONS

Simmer zucchini and onion together until almost tender. Mix together crackers and melted butter. Layer all ingredients together in a buttered baking dish, beginning with cracker mixture and ending with cheese. Bake at 375 degrees for 30 minutes until bubbly and lightly browned.

Zucchini Slippers

This dish is from Turkey, where it is called "little slippers." It can be served as a side dish or cut into small squares and served as an appetizer with toothpicks.

INGREDIENTS

3 medium zucchini
2 eggs, beaten (or ½ cup egg substitute)
1½ cups shredded cheddar cheese
½ cup cottage cheese (fat-free works fine)
2 Tbsp. chopped parsley
½ tsp. salt
dash of pepper

SERVES
6

DIRECTIONS

Cut off ends of zucchini and cook whole in boiling, salted water about 12 minutes, until tender but still firm. Drain and cut zucchini in half lengthwise. Scoop out seeds, leaving a boat. Mix together remaining ingredients. Fill each shell and arrange in a greased baking dish. Bake uncovered for 15 minutes at 350 degrees. Broil until lightly browned and cheese has melted.

Zucchini Carrot Au Gratin

This combination of zucchini, carrots, and Swiss cheese is perfect when you want a warm and satisfying side dish.

INGREDIENTS

3 cups sliced carrots
7 cups sliced zucchini
¼ cup butter or stick margarine, cut into small pieces
1 tsp. salt
½ tsp. pepper
1 cup shredded Swiss cheese
½ cup chicken broth

SERVES
8

DIRECTIONS

Cook carrots in boiling salted water for about 5 minutes. Drain. Layer zucchini and carrots in a greased 9x13 baking dish and dot with butter. Sprinkle with salt and pepper. Cover with cheese. Pour broth over top and cover with foil. Bake at 350 degrees for 20 minutes. Remove foil and bake 20 minutes until cheese is browned and melted.

Baked Zucchini Sticks

Only two ingredients, but these tasty treats are perfect for a barbecue or simple side dish.

INGREDIENTS

3 medium zucchini, cut into ½-inch sticks
salt

SERVES
4–6

DIRECTIONS

Place zucchini on well-greased baking sheet. Sprinkle with salt and bake at 400 degrees for about 10 minutes. Turn, sprinkle with more salt, and bake until crisp tender.

That Is One Big Zucchini!

Mr. John Evans of Alaska has created a living out of growing giant vegetables. He has held nine Guinness World Records for vegetables. In 1998, John grew a fifty-nine-pound zucchini, an Alaska state record at the time. John has won numerous ribbons for his giant veggies. He and wife, Mary, watch over them like children, even naming one huge zucchini Baby and putting a blanket on it at night to stave off the chill.

Bernard Lavery is world renowned for growing giant vegetables. He held the U.K. record for the largest marrow at 108 pounds 2 ounces in 1990.

In 2003 Sher Singh Kanwal of Niagara Falls, New York, grew the world's longest zucchini measuring 6 feet 4 inches. Hollowed out, it would make a nice canoe!

Green and Gold Zucchini Oven Frittata

This baked dish is best served warm or at room temperature.

SERVES 6

INGREDIENTS

1 onion, chopped
2 Tbsp. oil
2 medium zucchini, grated
2 medium yellow squash, grated
2 Tbsp. chopped fresh parsley
½ tsp. salt
½ tsp. oregano

¼ tsp. pepper
3 eggs, beaten (or ¾ cup egg substitute)
½ cup milk (fat-free works fine)
1 cup shredded cheddar cheese
½ cup saltine cracker crumbs

DIRECTIONS

Sauté onion in oil until tender. Remove from heat and add zucchini, yellow squash, parsley, spices, eggs, and milk. Put half the mixture in a buttered 9x13 baking dish. Sprinkle with half the cheese and half the crumbs. Spoon other half of zucchini mixture on top. Sprinkle with remaining crumbs and cheese. Bake at 325 degrees for 45 minutes.

Italian Zucchini Quiche

Tasty and filling, this dish is perfect for brunch, and it also travels well. I love to bring this to potlucks.

INGREDIENTS

4 cups sliced zucchini
¾ cup onions, chopped
¼ cup margarine
2 Tbsp. chopped fresh parsley
¼ tsp. salt
½ tsp. pepper
¼ tsp. garlic powder
¼ tsp. basil
¼ tsp. oregano
2 eggs, beaten (or ½ cup egg substitute)
2 cups shredded mozzarella cheese
1 unbaked piecrust

**SERVES
6–8**

DIRECTIONS

Brown zucchini and onions in margarine until tender. Add spices and toss to coat. Cook an additional 2 minutes. Combine eggs and cheese, and then add zucchini mixture. Pour into 9-inch pie plate lined with piecrust. Bake at 375 degrees for 25 minutes or until knife comes out clean. Serve warm.

Zucchini Custard Casserole

A light and fluffy side dish that is a great addition to brunch. If you like things extra spicy, you can add more hot pepper sauce.

INGREDIENTS

SERVES 4–6

5 medium zucchini, cubed
¼ cup butter or stick margarine, melted
3 eggs (or ¾ cup egg substitute)
½ cup evaporated milk (fat-free works fine)
2 Tbsp. dry bread crumbs
1 tsp. dried minced onions
1 tsp. Worcestershire sauce
1 dash liquid hot pepper sauce
¾ tsp. salt
⅛ tsp. pepper
⅓ cup grated Parmesan cheese

DIRECTIONS

Sauté zucchini in melted butter until tender. In a large bowl, mix together eggs, milk, bread crumbs, onions, seasonings, and 2 tablespoons cheese. Fold in zucchini. Place in buttered 1½-quart casserole dish. Sprinkle remaining cheese on top. Bake at 350 degrees for 40 minutes.

GET A RISE

No yeast necessary in these luscious loaves

Zucchini Bread

This traditional sweet bread has been a favorite for decades. For many people, it's the only way they've eaten our versatile green friend.

INGREDIENTS

MAKES
2
LOAVES

3 eggs (or ¾ cup egg substitute)
1 cup oil
2 cups sugar
2 cups grated zucchini
3 tsp. vanilla
3 cups flour
1 tsp. baking soda

½ tsp. baking powder
¼ tsp. cloves
3 tsp. cinnamon
1 tsp. salt
¼ tsp. nutmeg
1 cup chopped nuts (optional)

DIRECTIONS

Beat eggs until foamy. Add oil, sugar, zucchini, and vanilla, and mix well. Stir together flour, baking soda, baking powder, and spices. Add zucchini mixture and blend well. Fold in nuts. Pour into 2 well-greased 8x4 loaf pans. Bake at 350 degrees for about 1 hour.

Zucchini Pumpkin Bread

A wonderful mix of spices and flavors, this bread is perfect for sharing. My neighbors enjoy it during the holidays.

INGREDIENTS

1 cup butter or stick margarine
2 cups sugar
3 eggs, beaten (or ¾ cup egg substitute)
1 Tbsp. vanilla
1 cup grated zucchini
1 cup canned pumpkin
3 cups flour

1 tsp. baking soda
½ tsp. baking powder
½ tsp. salt
½ tsp. cinnamon
½ tsp. nutmeg
½ tsp. cloves
1 cup chopped nuts

MAKES
2
LOAVES

DIRECTIONS

Cream together butter and sugar. Add eggs, vanilla, zucchini, and pumpkin, and mix well. Combine other ingredients and then add to creamed mixture. Blend well and pour into 2 greased 8x4 loaf pans. Bake at 350 degrees for 45 minutes or until toothpick comes out clean.

Zucchini Coconut Carrot Muffins

I love serving these warm on a fall morning. Mixture can also be baked in loaf pans and served like bread.

MAKES
12
LARGE
MUFFINS

INGREDIENTS

4 eggs, beaten (or 1 cup egg substitute)
2 Tbsp. butter or stick margarine
2 cups sugar
1 cup oil
1 tsp. vanilla
2¾ cups flour
1 cup shredded coconut
2 tsp. cinnamon

1 tsp. nutmeg
2 tsp. baking powder
½ tsp. baking soda
¼ tsp. salt
2½ cups grated zucchini
½ cup grated carrots
½ cup chopped pecans

DIRECTIONS

Beat together eggs, butter, sugar, oil, and vanilla. In a separate bowl, mix together flour, coconut, spices, salt, baking powder, and soda. Add to egg mixture and blend well. Fold in zucchini and carrots. Fill well-greased muffin tins ¾ full. Sprinkle nuts on top. Bake at 375 degrees for 25 minutes.

Zucchini Pancakes

Moist and hearty, these pancakes can be served with jam or syrup, or with salt, pepper, and sour cream.

INGREDIENTS

2 cups finely grated zucchini
3 Tbsp. oil
4 eggs, beaten (or 1 cup egg substitute)
¾ cup flour
1 tsp. sugar
½ tsp. salt
4 tsp. baking powder
¼ cup melted butter or stick margarine

SERVES
4–6

DIRECTIONS

Beat together zucchini, oil, and eggs. Stir together dry ingredients, and then add to zucchini mixture. Blend well. Spoon batter onto hot, greased griddle. Cook until bubbles cover top. Then turn and cook until done. Brush with melted butter.

Zucchini Orange Bread

A moist and sunny bread that is a great start for the day.

INGREDIENTS

MAKES 2 LOAVES

4 eggs, well beaten (or 1 cup egg substitute)
1½ cups sugar
¾ cup oil
⅔ cup orange juice
2 tsp. orange zest
2 cups grated zucchini
3¼ cups flour
1½ tsp. baking powder

1½ tsp. baking soda
1 tsp. salt
2½ tsp. cinnamon
½ tsp. cloves
½ cup chopped nuts (optional)

Glaze:
1 cup powdered sugar
2–3 Tbsp. orange juice

DIRECTIONS

Beat eggs. Add sugar, oil, juice, zest, and zucchini. Mix well. Combine dry ingredients and add to zucchini mixture. Mix well. Place in greased 8x4 loaf pans. Bake at 350 degrees for 45 minutes, or until toothpick comes out clean. In a bowl, stir together powdered sugar and just enough orange juice to make a glaze. Drizzle over bread when cool.

Blackberry Zucchini Bread

The orange flavor gives this bread a tangy twist.

INGREDIENTS

1 cup butter or stick margarine

2 cups sugar

3 eggs, beaten (or ¾ cup egg substitute)

1 Tbsp. vanilla

1 cup grated zucchini

1 (16.5-oz.) can blackberries, drained (or 8-oz. package of frozen)

½ cup orange juice

1 Tbsp. orange zest

3 cups flour

1 tsp. baking soda

½ tsp. baking powder

½ tsp. salt

MAKES 2 LOAVES

DIRECTIONS

Cream together butter and sugar. Add eggs and vanilla and beat well. Mix in zucchini, juice, zest, and blackberries. Stir together dry ingredients and add in, mixing well. Place in greased 8x4 loaf pans and bake at 350 degrees for 45 minutes or until toothpick comes out clean.

Hawaiian Zucchini Bread

Fruits and nuts give a sweet crunchy flavor you'll love.

INGREDIENTS

3 eggs, beaten (or ¾ cup egg substitute)
2 cups sugar
2 tsp. vanilla
1 cup oil
3 cups grated zucchini
½ cup raisins
1 cup crushed pineapple, drained
1 cup chopped pecans
3 cups flour
1 tsp. baking powder
1 tsp. baking soda
½ tsp. salt

MAKES
2
LOAVES

DIRECTIONS

Combine eggs, sugar, vanilla, and oil. Add zucchini, raisins, pineapple, and pecans. Mix well. Stir together dry ingredients and then add to zucchini mixture. Mix well and pour into greased 8x4 loaf pans. Bake at 350 degrees for 50 minutes or until toothpick comes out clean.

Zucchini Green Chili Corn Bread

I love making this bread for barbecues. It's the perfect complement!

INGREDIENTS

2 cups corn meal
2 cups flour
½ cup sugar
2 Tbsp. baking powder
2 tsp. salt
2 cups skim milk
⅔ cup oil
2 eggs, beaten (or ½ cup egg substitute)
1 (7-oz.) can diced green chilies
2 cups grated zucchini, drained well

SERVES
12

DIRECTIONS

Combine corn meal, flour, sugar, baking powder, and salt. In a separate bowl, combine milk, oil, eggs, chilies, and zucchini. Add to dry mixture and stir just until blended. Pour into greased 9x13 baking pan. Bake for 25 minutes or until toothpick comes out clean.

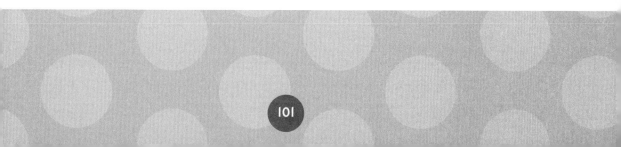

Sweet Zucchini Corn Bread

Extra moist, this corn bread can be served at breakfast or as a sweet addition with your favorite chili.

INGREDIENTS

2 cups corn meal
2 cups flour
½ cup sugar
2 Tbsp. baking powder
2 tsp. salt
2 cups skim milk
⅔ cup oil

2 eggs, beaten (or ½ cup egg substitute)
½ cup honey
2 cups grated zucchini, drained well
¼ cup honey
¼ cup soft butter

SERVES 12

DIRECTIONS

Combine corn meal, flour, sugar, baking powder, and salt. In a separate bowl, combine milk, oil, eggs, honey, and zucchini. Add to dry mixture and stir just until blended. Pour into greased 9x13 pan. Bake for 25 minutes or until toothpick comes out clean.

Combine honey and butter. Spread on top, and let it melt into the bread. Serve warm.

Easy Cake Mix Zucchini Bread

See if anyone notices a difference. I make this almost weekly.

INGREDIENTS

2 cups grated zucchini
1 box spice or carrot cake mix
3 eggs (or ¾ cup egg substitute)
¼ cup oil

⅓ cup sugar (or baking sugar substitute)
½ cup chopped nuts (optional)

MAKES
2
LOAVES

DIRECTIONS

Mix all ingredients together and place in well greased or lined 8x4 loaf pans. Bake at 350 degrees for about 45 minutes.

"Did you hear about the lady who grew the world's largest zucchini? It was so big, it stuck out the hatch, and she couldn't lock the car. Then she stopped for some things at the store, and when she came back to her car, something terrible had happened. Somebody had left her the second-largest zucchini, too!"

Chocolate Nut Zucchini Bread

Super moist—and the glaze makes it even sweeter!

INGREDIENTS

MAKES 2 LOAVES

3 eggs, beaten (or ¾ cup egg substitute)
2 cups sugar (or baking sugar substitute)
¾ cup oil
½ cup buttermilk
2 cups grated zucchini
¼ cup cocoa
2½ tsp. baking soda
1 tsp. salt
1 tsp. vanilla

2 cups flour
1 cup chopped nuts

Glaze:
1 cup powdered sugar
2 Tbsp. soft butter
1 tsp. vanilla
2–3 Tbsp. milk

DIRECTIONS

Beat together eggs, sugar, oil, and buttermilk. Add zucchini and mix well. Combine dry ingredients and add to egg mixture. Blend well and pour into greased 8x4 loaf pans. Bake at 350 degrees for 45 minutes or until toothpick comes out clean. Cool.

Whisk together butter, vanilla, and powdered sugar. Add milk by teaspoonfuls until mixture forms a glaze. Spread over top of loaves.

Honey Zucchini Bread

The combination of spice and honey make this bread extra special.

INGREDIENTS

3 eggs, well beaten (or ¾ cup egg substitute)
1 cup oil
1 cup honey
1 Tbsp. vanilla
2 cups grated zucchini
3 cups flour

1 tsp. baking powder
1 tsp. baking soda
1 tsp. salt
1½ tsp. cinnamon
1 tsp. ginger
½ tsp. nutmeg
1 cup chopped nuts

MAKES
2
LOAVES

DIRECTIONS

Beat together eggs, oil, honey, and vanilla. Mix in zucchini. In a separate bowl, stir together dry ingredients. Add to zucchini mixture. Blend well. Mix in nuts. Pour into well-greased 8x4 loaf pans. Bake at 350 degrees for 45 minutes or until toothpick comes out clean.

HOW SWEET IT IS

Zucchini makes cakes, cookies, and desserts moist and mouthwatering

The Zucchini's Charitable Contributions

Seven miles east of Gainesville, Florida, on County Road 234, you'll find the town of Windsor.

In 1981, a group of Windsorites gathered to discuss the need for a firehouse. They had a fire truck but nowhere to store it. They were lucky to have the land donated. A generous banker from the town of Live Oak arranged the financing for the new building. But that didn't erase the annual payment of $1,800.

For a small town with a volunteer fire department, they would have to find a way to raise the money each year to pay off the loan. The same ambitious group who found the land and loan decided to start a festival. They would celebrate something they had plenty of as well as an overabundance of interest.

They organized the first Windsor Zucchini Festival. They organized contests, entertainment, and of course, plenty of wonderful green food. With the exception of three years, the festival has been an annual event, and the ten-year mortgage on the building was paid off three years early. They continue to hold the festival each year to support their small local fire department.

Zucchini Spice Cake

This cake is wonderful served warm. It is moist and has a wonderful orangey zest.

INGREDIENTS

SERVES 8–10

1½ cups oil
2 eggs (or ½ cup egg substitute)
2 cups brown sugar
3 cups flour
1 tsp. soda
1 tsp. salt
2 tsp. cinnamon

1 tsp. nutmeg
½ tsp. cloves
1 tsp. vanilla
3 cups grated zucchini
1 Tbsp. grated orange peel
Powdered sugar or whipped topping

DIRECTIONS

Cream together oil, eggs, and brown sugar. In a separate bowl, sift together flour, soda, salt, cinnamon, nutmeg, and cloves. Mix into creamed mixture. Add vanilla, zucchini, and orange peel. Mix well. Bake in a greased and floured tube or bundt pan at 350 degrees for 1¼–1½ hours. Cool. Serve with a dusting of powdered sugar or a dollop of whipped topping.

Nutty Zucchini Cake

The sugar in the pan gives this moist cake a light glaze after baking.

INGREDIENTS

SERVES 8–12

3 cups grated and strained zucchini
3 cups sugar (or baking sugar substitute)
3 cups flour
4 eggs (or 1 cup egg substitute)
1½ cups oil
1 cup chopped nuts
1 tsp. baking soda
1½ tsp. cinnamon
2 tsp. baking powder
½ tsp. salt

DIRECTIONS

Mix all ingredients together. Grease a bundt pan with shortening, and then sprinkle entire pan with sugar. Bake at 350 degrees for 1 hour. Cool and invert on serving plate.

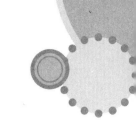

Zucchini Dessert Quiche

It's fluffy and sweet, and there is no need for a crust.

INGREDIENTS

2 eggs well beaten (or ½ cup egg substitute)
1½ cups evaporated milk (fat-free works fine)
1¼ cups sugar (or baking sugar substitute)
1 tsp. cinnamon
½ tsp. nutmeg
¼ tsp. salt
2 cups peeled, boiled, and mashed zucchini

**SERVES
8**

DIRECTIONS

Beat together eggs, milk, sugar, and spices. Add zucchini and mix well. Pour into a greased pie plate. Bake at 400 degrees for about 40 minutes or until set.

Zucchini Nut Drop Cookies

I love these wholesome and moist cookies when they've cooled because they are so chewy.

INGREDIENTS

1 cup sugar (or baking sugar substitute)
½ cup shortening
1 egg (or ¼ cup egg substitute)
1 cup grated zucchini
2 cups flour
1 tsp. baking soda
1 tsp. cinnamon
½ cup chopped nuts
½ cup raisins

**MAKES
3
DOZEN**

DIRECTIONS

Beat together sugar and shortening. Add egg and zucchini, and beat well. Sift together flour, soda, and cinnamon. Add to egg mixture. Fold in nuts and raisins. Drop from a teaspoon onto greased baking sheet. Bake at 375 degrees for 12–15 minutes.

Zucchini "Apple" Crisp

Serve this and sit back. When the compliments come pouring in, then you can reveal that there is not an apple in sight!

INGREDIENTS

1 extra large zucchini
2 Tbsp. lemon juice
2 Tbsp. sugar
½ tsp. cinnamon
½ cup brown sugar
½ cup rolled oats
¼ cup flour
¼ cup butter or stick margarine

SERVES 4–6

DIRECTIONS

Peel zucchini so that no green is left showing. Cut in half lengthwise. Remove seeds and slice in ¼-inch half moons to look like apple slices. Place slices in ziplock plastic bag and sprinkle with lemon juice. Shake to coat. Combine sugar and cinnamon. Add to bag and shake well. Place zucchini slices in buttered 8x8 baking dish. Combine brown sugar, oats, and flour. Cut in butter. Sprinkle over zucchini slices. Bake at 350 degrees for 40–45 minutes. Serve warm with ice cream or whipped topping.

Zucchini Chocolate Chip Cookies

These cookies are soft and cakelike. The chocolate and cinnamon are a tasty combination.

INGREDIENTS

¾ cup shortening
1 cup sugar (or baking sugar substitute)
1 egg (or ¼ cup egg substitute)
1 tsp. vanilla
2½ cups flour
2 tsp. baking powder
½ tsp. salt
1 tsp. cinnamon
1½ cups grated zucchini
1 cup chocolate chips

MAKES
3
DOZEN

DIRECTIONS

Cream together shortening, sugar, egg, and vanilla. In a separate bowl, combine flour, baking powder, salt, and cinnamon. Add to creamed mixture. Add zucchini and chocolate chips. Drop from a teaspoon onto ungreased baking sheet. Bake at 350 degrees for about 15 minutes.

Honey and Spice Zucchini Pie

This pie is a holiday favorite. Pumpkin pie will take a backseat!

INGREDIENTS

1 unbaked pie crust
2 cups zucchini, cooked, pureed, and strained
¼ cup honey
⅓ cup sugar
1 tsp. salt
2 tsp. cinnamon
1 tsp. ginger
¼ tsp. allspice
½ tsp. nutmeg
1 (13 oz.) can evaporated milk (fat-free works fine)
2 eggs, beaten (or ¼ cup egg substitute)

SERVES
8

DIRECTIONS

Mix together zucchini, honey, sugar, and spices. In a saucepan, warm milk and add to zucchini mixture. Stir in eggs and blend well. Pour into unbaked pie shell. Bake at 425 degrees for 15 minutes. Reduce oven to 350 degrees and bake another 40 minutes or until knife inserted in center comes out clean. Cool for several hours. Serve with whipped topping.

Chocolate Buttermilk Zucchini Cake

Super moist. The chocolate chips make the perfect frosting.

INGREDIENTS

1 cup brown sugar
½ cup butter or stick margarine
½ cup sugar
½ cup oil
3 eggs (or ¾ cup egg substitute)
1 tsp. vanilla

1 cup buttermilk
2½ cups flour
1 tsp. cinnamon
2 tsp. baking soda
4 Tbsp. cocoa
2 cups grated zucchini

SERVES
12

DIRECTIONS

In a large bowl, cream together brown sugar, butter, sugar, and oil. Mix in eggs, vanilla, and buttermilk. In a separate bowl, mix together flour, cinnamon, baking soda, and cocoa. Add to creamed mixture. Stir in zucchini. Mix until all ingredients are well combined.

Pour into a greased and floured 9x13 pan. Sprinkle top with chocolate chips. Bake at 325 degrees for 45 minutes. Turn off oven and let cake cool inside. Cake will seem very moist. Serve with whipped topping.

Zucchini Cream Cheese Bars

I add a drop of green food coloring in the frosting—just to remind everyone that this dessert has a special ingredient.

INGREDIENTS

3 eggs (or ¾ cup egg substitute)
2 cups sugar (or baking sugar substitute)
1 cup oil
2 cups grated zucchini
3 tsp. vanilla
2½ cups flour
¼ tsp. baking powder
1 tsp. salt
2 tsp. baking soda

Frosting:
½ cup butter, softened
1 (3-oz.) package cream cheese
1 tsp. vanilla
2½ cups powdered sugar
milk as needed

MAKES ONE DOZEN

DIRECTIONS

Beat together eggs, sugar, and oil. Add zucchini and vanilla. Mix together dry ingredients and then combine with zucchini mixture. Mix until combined well. Pour into a greased and floured 9x13 baking dish. Bake at 350 degrees for 25 minutes or until toothpick comes out clean. Cool.

For frosting: Combine butter and cream cheese and beat until light. Add vanilla and powdered sugar. Beat until fluffy, adding a slight amount of milk for consistency. Frost bars when they are completely cool.

Zucchini Carrot Cookies

Sweet and moist—the perfect cookie for an afternoon snack!

INGREDIENTS

¾ cup butter or stick margarine
¾ cup sugar (or baking sugar substitute)
1 egg (or ¼ cup egg substitute)
1 tsp. vanilla
2½ cups flour
2 tsp. baking powder
½ tsp. baking soda
2 tsp. cinnamon
1 cup grated carrots
1 cup grated zucchini

MAKES
3
DOZEN

DIRECTIONS

Cream butter and sugar. Add egg and vanilla, and mix well. Add the zucchini and carrots. In a separate bowl, combine dry ingredients. Add to creamed mixture and mix well. Drop from a teaspoon onto ungreased baking sheet. Bake at 350 degrees for about 11 minutes.

Green Surprise Cookies

Lots of good stuff in these. Kids love them.

INGREDIENTS

½ cup butter or stick margarine
¾ cup sugar (or baking sugar substitute)
1 egg (or ¼ cup egg substitute)
½ tsp. vanilla
1½ cups flour
1 tsp. cinnamon
½ tsp. baking soda
½ tsp. salt
1 cup rolled oats
1 cup chopped nuts
1 cup grated zucchini
½ cup chocolate chips (sugar free will work)
½ cup butterscotch chips (sugar free will work)

MAKES
3
DOZEN

DIRECTIONS

Beat together butter and sugar until fluffy. Add eggs and vanilla, and beat well. In a separate bowl, mix flour, cinnamon, baking soda, and salt. Add to butter mixture. Beat until blended. Add oats, nuts, zucchini, and both chips. Drop from a teaspoon onto ungreased baking sheet. Bake at 350 degrees for about 11 minutes.

Zucchini Oatmeal Cookies

Sweet and tasty, but healthy too. I take these along when I hike or ski. They are a perfect wholesome snack.

INGREDIENTS

½ cup shortening
¾ cup honey
1 egg (or ¼ cup egg substitute)
2 cups flour
1 cup oatmeal
1 tsp. baking soda

1 tsp. cinnamon
½ tsp. nutmeg
¼ tsp. salt
1 cup grated zucchini
1 cup raisins

MAKES
3
DOZEN

DIRECTIONS

Cream together shortening and honey. Add egg and beat well. In a separate bowl, stir together dry ingredients. Add alternately with zucchini to creamed mixture. Fold in raisins. Drop from a teaspoon onto greased baking sheet. Bake at 375 degrees for 11 minutes.

Zucchini Brownies

So moist, you'll never make brownies any other way. The marshmallows in the frosting make it extra sweet and fluffy. While I try to offer fat-free versions, you need real butter and milk for this one!

INGREDIENTS

SERVES 12

2 cups grated zucchini
1½ cups sugar
¾ cup oil
2 tsp. vanilla
2 cups flour
⅓ cup cocoa
1½ tsp. baking soda
1 tsp. salt
½ cup nuts (optional)

Frosting:

¼ cup butter
1 cup sugar
¼ cup milk
½ cup chocolate chips
½ cup miniature marshmallows
1 tsp. vanilla
½ cup chopped nuts (optional)

DIRECTIONS

Combine zucchini, sugar, oil, and vanilla. Mix dry ingredients and add to zucchini mixture. Pour into greased 9x13 baking pan. Bake at 350 degrees for 35 to 40 minutes. Cool.

For frosting: In a saucepan, melt butter on medium heat. Add sugar and milk. Bring to a boil, stirring frequently. Cook and stir about 1 minute. Remove from heat. Add chocolate chips and marshmallows. Stir until melted. Add vanilla. Spread over brownies. Sprinkle with nuts.

Pineapple-Coconut Zucchini Cake

This moist cake is a tropical treat. I love it for a light summer dessert.

INGREDIENTS

3 eggs, beaten (or ¾ cup egg substitute)
2 cups sugar (or baking sugar substitute)
1 cup oil
2 tsp. vanilla
3 cups flour
1 tsp. baking powder
1 tsp. salt
1 tsp. baking soda
1 cup crushed pineapple, drained
½ cup raisins
1 cup chopped pecans
1 cup shredded coconut
2½ cups grated zucchini

SERVES
12

DIRECTIONS

Beat together eggs, sugar, oil, and vanilla. In a separate bowl, mix flour, baking powder, salt, and soda. Add to egg mixture and mix well. Add remaining ingredients and mix thoroughly. Pour into a greased 9x13 baking pan and bake at 350 degrees for 1 hour or until toothpick comes out clean. Dust with powdered sugar before serving.

Zucchini Ice Cream

I add green food coloring just to give it a zuke effect. But with this sweet and creamy treat, no one will believe it is packed full of veggie goodness!

INGREDIENTS

SERVES 8

1 envelope Knox unflavored gelatin
½ cup cold water
3 cups peeled and grated zucchini
1 cup honey
2 (13-oz.) cans evaporated milk
2 tsp. vanilla
enough whole milk (or cream) to make 8 cups
green food coloring (if desired)

DIRECTIONS

Soften gelatin in water. Simmer zucchini in honey until tender. Stir in softened gelatin. Add evaporated milk and vanilla. Mix well. Add milk to make 8 cups. Add a few drops of green food coloring, if desired. Mix well. Cover and chill for 4–5 hours. Beat well with the electric mixer. Pour into a mold (or 8x4 loaf pan); cover and freeze until "mushy." Remove from freezer and beat until smooth. Return to mold and cover with wax paper. Freeze until firm.

IN A PICKLE

Zucchini is great dilled or sweet, in relishes, or in other pleasing preserves.

Zucchini Fridge Pickles

No messing with canning these fresh and easy pickles. Just store them in the fridge, and they are ready to enjoy.

INGREDIENTS

MAKES
2
PINTS

1¼ cups water
1¼ cups apple cider vinegar
1 tsp. salt
2 tsp. mustard seeds
1 Tbsp. black pepper corns
4 small firm zucchini, sliced in ½-inch rounds
1 medium onion, sliced
2 garlic cloves, minced
1 red bell pepper, seeded and cut into 1-inch chunks
2 Tbsp. chopped fresh dill weed

DIRECTIONS

In a large saucepan combine water, vinegar, salt, mustard seeds, and peppercorns. Bring to a boil and cook 10 minutes. In a large bowl, combine remaining ingredients. Pour hot liquid over vegetables. Mix well and cover tightly. Let mixture sit at room temperature for 4 hours. Chill thoroughly before serving. It will last a month in the fridge.

Zucchini Sweet Pickles

Sweet and tasty—another of my mother's classic recipes.

INGREDIENTS

3 cups sliced zucchini
½ cup chopped onions
1 large red bell pepper, seeded and cut in 1-inch chunks
1 Tbsp. salt
1 cup sugar
¾ cup white vinegar
¾ tsp. mustard seeds
¾ tsp. celery seeds
¼ tsp. dry mustard

MAKES
2
PINTS

DIRECTIONS

Mix vegetables in a large bowl. Sprinkle with salt. Cover and chill for 1 hour. Drain. In a large saucepan, combine sugar, vinegar, mustard seeds, celery seeds, and dry mustard. Bring to boil. Add vegetables and return to a boil. Remove from heat and spoon into small jars or plastic containers. Cool completely, and chill at least 24 hours until serving. It will last up to a month in the refrigerator. They can also be frozen.

Zucchini Relish

I love this over fish or pork chops.

INGREDIENTS

5 large zucchini, peeled and chopped
5 large onions, chopped
3 green peppers, seeded and chopped
3 red peppers, seeded and chopped
½ cup salt
1 Tbsp. alum

ice cubes (about 25)
5 cups vinegar
5 cups sugar
2 Tbsp. celery seed
2 Tbsp. mustard seed
1 Tbsp. turmeric

MAKES 6 PINTS

DIRECTIONS

Mix vegetables together in a large bowl. Sprinkle with salt and alum. Cover with ice cubes. Let sit for one hour. Drain. In a large saucepan, mix vinegar, sugar, celery seed, mustard seed, and turmeric. Bring to a boil, add vegetables, and cook until clear. Ladle into clean, pint jars leaving ½-inch headspace. Wipe rims and adjust lids. Process jars in boiling water bath for 10 minutes. Start timing after water boils.

Zucchini Marmalade

Sweet and unique. This makes a great housewarming or hostess gift.

INGREDIENTS

6 cups peeled and finely grated zucchini
1 cup water
6 cups sugar
2 Tbsp. lemon juice
1 (20-oz.) can crushed pineapple
1 (3-oz.) box apricot gelatin

MAKES 3 PINTS

DIRECTIONS

In a saucepan, bring zucchini and water to a boil. Gently boil for 10 minutes. Add sugar, lemon juice, and pineapple. Cook another 10 minutes. Stir in gelatin and cook 10 minutes more. Ladle into hot, sterile jars. Wipe tops and adjust lids. Cool completely.

Zucchini Lemon Curd

This is wonderful spooned over angel food cake or ice cream.

INGREDIENTS

6 medium zucchini
2 cups sugar
½ cup butter (not margarine)
2 lemons, juiced and zested

MAKES
3½
PINTS

DIRECTIONS

Peel and seed zucchini and cut in large chunks. Boil in unsalted water for about 10 minutes until tender. Puree in blender. In a double boiler, cook zucchini, sugar, butter, lemon juice, and lemon zest for about 15 minutes or until thick and creamy. Ladle into hot, sterilized jars. Wipe rims and adjust lids. Water bath jars for 10 minutes. Cool completely.

Zucchini Pineapple

Use as you would crushed pineapple. This is a great way to use your bounty and save money in the process. As with most zucchini recipes, you can't tell the difference!

INGREDIENTS

3 cups sugar
½ cup lemon juice
6 cups pineapple juice
18 cups peeled and finely grated zucchini

MAKES
12
PINTS

DIRECTIONS

Bring sugar and juices to a boil. Add zucchini and simmer for 20 minutes. Ladle into hot, sterile jars. Wipe rims and adjust lids. Water bath jars for 10 minutes. Cool completely.

Still wondering what to do with your overload of green marvels?

Here are some creative suggestions I've gathered over the years to utilize zucchini that you may not have thought about.

1. Hollow a large one out and use it as a bike helmet.
2. Send them to school with your children to give to their teachers instead of apples.
3. Give the extra large ones to your mechanic as tire stops.
4. Put an extra large one in your toilet tank to save water.
5. Paint faces on them and sell them as "pet zucchini."
6. Use them as bowling pins.
7. Use them to roll out pie dough.
8. Practice your shot-put throw.
9. Put them in a basket on your porch as a deterrent to door-to-door solicitors.
10. Donate them to the street department to fill potholes.

Zucchini Pâté

Perfect with crackers as a special dip for parties.

INGREDIENTS

SERVES
4–6

1 medium zucchini, grated
1 tsp. white vinegar
1 tsp. salt
1 tsp. sugar
2 Tbsp. chopped fresh parsley
2 Tbsp. chopped fresh chives
1 (3-oz.) package cream cheese (light cream cheese works fine)
¼ tsp. salt
¼ tsp. pepper
paprika

DIRECTIONS

Mix zucchini with vinegar, salt and sugar. Put it in cheesecloth or a colander and let sit for 1 hour. Strain zucchini to get as much moisture out as possible. In a food processor or blender, finely chop parsley and chives. Add zucchini and process until smooth. Add cream cheese, salt, and pepper. Process until well mixed. Scoop into serving dish and chill at least 2 hours. Sprinkle with paprika right before serving.

Zucchini Salsa

This salsa is tasty and always goes quick at my house. Besides the chopping, it's a super simple recipe.

INGREDIENTS

10 cups finely chopped zucchini
3 cups finely chopped onion
25 Anaheim chilies, finely chopped
5 Tbsp. salt
5 cups chopped tomatoes
2 cups cider vinegar
1 cup brown sugar
1 Tbsp. corn starch

1 Tbsp. crushed red pepper flakes
1 Tbsp. cumin
2 tsp. dry mustard
1 tsp. pepper
1 tsp. turmeric
1 tsp. garlic powder
1 tsp. nutmeg

MAKES 3 QUARTS

DIRECTIONS

Combine zucchini, onion, chilies, and salt in a large bowl and refrigerate overnight. The next day, rinse through a colander and squeeze out as much moisture as possible. Use towels to pat dry.

Add other ingredients to zucchini mixture in a large kettle and mix well. Bring to a boil and reduce heat. Simmer for 30 minutes. Pour into jars and refrigerate.

A BLOSSOMING SIGN OF SPRING

Tender flowers signal a new beginning. Their fresh and delicate taste is satisfying but keeps you anticipating what is yet to come.

Crispy Fried Zucchini Blossoms

This is a zucchini festival favorite, but why not enjoy it anytime?

INGREDIENTS

12 zucchini blossoms
⅔ cup flour
¾ cup club soda (or beer)
Oil for deep frying

SERVES
4–6

DIRECTIONS

Whisk flour into soda (or beer) until smooth. Carefully dip each blossom in batter to thinly coat. Fry 2 to 3 blossoms at a time in a deep fryer or a saucepan in 1-inch of hot (375 degrees) oil. Drain on paper towels and season with salt.

The Blossom Quandary

When I stand at the gate of my garden in the late spring and marvel at the golden flowers peeking through the large dark leaves, I have torturous thoughts about whether to pick them or wait until they have attained all their green glory. But then it struck me—this isn't nipping them in the bud, but rather a tantalizing way to anticipate what is to come. Picking and enjoying the blossoms is a wonderful alternative to being inundated with thigh-sized fruit later in the summer. The blossoms are delicate and delicious, and when you enjoy them, you can't help but ponder the succulent fruit that is soon to follow.

Tuscan Stuffed Baby Zucchini Blossoms

This recipe uses blossoms still attached to baby zucchini. It is as unique as it is flavorful.

SERVES 6–8

INGREDIENTS

5 Tbsp. extra-virgin olive oil
1 large onion, finely chopped
1 cup plain dry bread crumbs
1 Tbsp. chopped fresh thyme
1 cup seeded and finely chopped tomatoes
⅓ cup grated Parmesan cheese
2 eggs, beaten (or ½ cup egg substitute)
1 garlic clove, minced

¾ tsp. salt
¼ tsp. ground black pepper
16 female blossoms with baby zucchini attached
2 Tbsp. extra virgin olive oil
2 lemons cut into 8 wedges each

DIRECTIONS

Heat oil in a large skillet over medium-high heat. Add onion and sauté about 5 minutes. Add bread crumbs and thyme, and stir until bread crumbs are lightly toasted, about 3 minutes. Transfer to a large bowl. Mix in tomatoes, cheese, eggs, garlic, salt, and pepper. Coat a large baking dish with about 1 tablespoon oil. Fill blossoms with bread crumb mixture, using about a tablespoon for each blossom. Sprinkle any remaining bread crumb mixture over baking dish. Place zucchini with blossoms carefully on top of bread crumbs in dish. Drizzle 2 tablespoons oil over top. Bake at 350 degrees about 30 minutes or until zucchini are fork tender. Serve with lemon wedges.

Crispy Curried Zucchini Blossoms

The curry adds just the right amount of spice to these crispy stuffed flowers. The cheese melts during frying and turns these blossoms into a decadent dish.

INGREDIENTS

SERVES 8

1 cup flour
2 tsp. curry powder
¼ tsp. salt
1 cup club soda, chilled
1 cup shredded mozzarella cheese
1 Tbsp. finely chopped fresh coriander (or ½ tsp. dried)
16 zucchini blossoms, pistils removed
oil

DIRECTIONS

Stir together flour, curry powder, and salt. Whisk in club soda until batter is smooth. Let the batter rest for 10 minutes. In a separate bowl, toss together cheese and coriander. Stuff each blossom with about 1 tablespoon of the mixture. Twist ends of the blossoms to seal. In a deep skillet, heat 1-inch oil to medium high. Working quickly in batches, dip blossoms in batter, coating them completely. Fry about 2 minutes on each side until they are golden and crisp. Drain on paper towel and sprinkle with salt.

Cheesy Stuffed Zucchini Blossoms

These delicate little pillows are mild and sweet. A perfect side dish or light dinner.

SERVES
6

INGREDIENTS

12 large zucchini blossoms
1 clove garlic, crushed
¼ tsp. salt
¾ cup ricotta cheese
¼ cup shredded mozzarella cheese
½ cup grated Parmesan cheese

¼ cup chopped fresh basil
½ tsp. pepper
1 egg, beaten (or ¼ cup egg
   substitute)
½ cup flour
Olive oil

DIRECTIONS

Remove pistils but leave stems in place. Mix together garlic, salt, cheeses, basil, and pepper. Carefully stuff each blossom with 1–2 tablespoons of cheese mixture. Twist tips of petals to seal. Dip each blossom in egg and then roll in flour. Heat oil in frying pan (about ½-inch deep) to medium high. Fry several blossoms at a time, turning occasionally until golden brown. Drain on paper towels.

Fried Feta Zucchini Blossoms

These crisp stuffed flowers have a wonderful tangy creaminess that will melt in your mouth.

INGREDIENTS

4 eggs (or 1 cup egg substitute)
2 cups dry bread crumbs
8 oz. feta cheese, cut into small cubes
18 zucchini blossoms
½ cup olive oil

**SERVES
6–8**

DIRECTIONS

Lightly beat eggs in a bowl. Place bread crumbs on a dish. Insert one cube of feta cheese into each zucchini blossom. Dredge blossoms in egg and then carefully roll in bread crumbs. Heat olive oil in a skillet over medium heat. Fry blossoms in skillet until golden brown. Drain on paper towels.

ABOUT THE AUTHOR

Brenda (Baumgartner) Stanley is a television news anchor and cooking show host for the NBC affiliate in Eastern Idaho. She has been recognized for her reporting by the Scripps Howard Foundation, the Hearst Journalism Awards, the Idaho Press Club, and the Society for Professional Journalists. She is a graduate of Dixie College in St. George, Utah, and the University of Utah in Salt Lake City. She is the mother of five children, including two sets of twins, and has two grandchildren. Brenda and her husband, Dave, a veterinarian, live on a small ranch near the Snake River with their horses and dogs.

What are you waiting for? They are growing by the minute.
Go. Pick. Prepare. Enjoy!